Racism and White Fragility

Black Lives Matter – Remembering George Floyd (I can't breathe!) Understanding Racism and its Impact on American Culture

By George DiAngelo

Table of Contents

Introduction to racism

Racism is the conviction that gatherings of people have diverse conduct qualities comparing to physical appearance and can be separated depending on the prevalence of one race over another. It might likewise mean partiality, segregation, or threat coordinated against others since they are of another race or ethnicity. Present-day variations of racism are regularly situated in a social view of natural contrasts between people groups. These perspectives can appear as social activities, practices or convictions, or political frameworks in which various races are positioned as innately better or substandard than one another, in light of assumed shared inheritable characteristics, capacities, or characteristics.

Regarding political frameworks (e.g., politically-sanctioned racial segregation) that help the declaration of partiality or revolution in unfair practices or laws, bigot philosophy may incorporate related social perspectives, for example, nativity, xenophobia, otherness, isolation, various leveled positioning, and supremacy.

While the ideas of race and ethnicity are viewed as independent in contemporary sociology, the two terms have a long history of equality in well-known utilization and more seasoned sociology writing. "Ethnicity" is frequently utilized one might say near one generally credited to "race": the division of human gatherings dependent on characteristics thought to be essential or inborn to the group (for example ordinary family or shared conduct). In this manner, racism and racial segregation are frequently used to portray separation on an ethnic or social premise, free of whether these distinctions are depicted as racial. As indicated by a United Nations show on racial segregation, there is no differentiation between the expressions "racial" and "ethnic" separation. The UN Convention further infers that prevalence dependent on racial separation is experimentally bogus, ethically condemnable, socially crooked and hazardous. The Convention additionally proclaimed that there is no legitimization for racial segregation, anyplace, in principle or practically speaking.

Racism is a moderately present day idea, emerging in the European period of dominion, the ensuing development of private enterprise, and particularly the Atlantic slave exchange, of which it was a significant main thrust. It was likewise a considerable power behind racial isolation particularly in the United States in the nineteenth and mid-twentieth hundreds of years and South Africa under politically-sanctioned racial segregation. Nineteenth and twentieth-century racism in Western culture is exceptionally very much recorded and comprises a reference point in studies and talks about racism. Racism has assumed a job in slaughters, for example, the Holocaust, the Armenian annihilation, and destruction of Serbs, and frontier ventures including the European colonization of the

Americas, Africa, and Asia just as the Soviet extraditions of indigenous minorities. Indigenous people groups have been—and are—frequently dependent upon supremacist perspectives.

In the nineteenth century, numerous researchers bought into the conviction that the human populace can be isolated into races. The term racism is a thing portraying the condition of being supremacist, i.e., buying into the opinion that the human populace can or ought to be characterized into races with differential capacities and demeanors. Which thus may spur a political belief system where rights and benefits are differentially appropriated dependent on racial classes. The inception of the root word "race" isn't apparent. Etymologists, for the most part, concur that it went to the English language from Middle French, yet there is no such concurrence on how it, for the most part, came into Latin-based dialects. An ongoing proposition is that it gets from the Arabic Ra's, which signifies "head, starting, beginning" or the Hebrew Rosh, which has a comparable significance. Early race scholars, by and large, held the view that a few races were second rate compared to other people and they, therefore, accepted that the differential treatment of races was legitimized entirely. These early speculations guided pseudo-logical research suppositions; the aggregate undertakings to sufficiently characterize and shape theories about racial contrasts are commonly named logical racism. However, this term is a misnomer, because of the absence of any real science backing the cases.

Today, most researcher, anthropologists, and sociologists dismiss a scientific classification of races for progressively explicit as well as experimentally accurate measures, for example, topography, ethnicity, or a past filled with endogamy. Until this point, there is little proof in human genome look into which demonstrates that race can be characterized to be valuable in deciding a hereditary grouping of people.

A section in the Oxford English Dictionary (2008) characterizes racialism as "[a]n prior term than racism, however now to a great extent supplanted by it", and refers to the expression "racialism" in a 1902 statement. The reexamined Oxford English Dictionary refers to the abbreviated term "racism" in a report from the next year, 1903. It was first characterized by the Oxford English Dictionary (second version, 1989) as "[t]he hypothesis that unmistakable human attributes and capacities are controlled by race"; a similar word reference named racism an equivalent of racialism: "confidence in the prevalence of a specific race". Before the finish of World War II, racism had gained similar supremacist undertones some time ago connected with racialism: racism currently suggested racial separation, racial supremacy, and a destructive expectation. (The expression "race contempt" had likewise been utilized by humanist Frederick Hertz in the late 1920s.)

As its history shows, the well-known utilization of the word racism is moderately later. The name came into across the board used in the Western world during the 1930s when it was utilized to portray the social and political belief system of Nazism, which rewarded "race" as a usually given political unit. It normally concurs that racism existed before the coinage of the word. However, there is certifiably not a broad concurrence on a solitary meaning of what racism is and what it isn't. Today, a few researchers of racism want to utilize the idea in the plural racisms, to stress its various structures that don't effectively fall under a single definition. They additionally contend that multiple types of racism have portrayed diverse, authentic periods and geological zones. Gather (2009: p. 11) sums up different existing meanings of racism and distinguishes three regular components contained in those meanings of racism. Initial, a chronicled, various leveled power connection between gatherings; second, a lot of thoughts (a belief system) about racial contrasts; and, third, oppressive activities (rehearses).

Lawful racism

Even though numerous nations around the world have passed laws identified with race and separation, the principal critical global human rights instrument created by the United Nations (UN) was the Universal Declaration of Human Rights (UDHR). Which was received by the United Nations General Assembly in 1948. The UDHR perceives that if individuals are to be treated with nobility, they require economic rights, social rights including training, and the rights to social and political interest and fundamental freedom. It further expresses that everybody is qualified for these rights "without differentiation of any sort, for example, race, shading, gender, language and religion, political or other supposition, national or social starting point, property, birth or different status".

The UN doesn't characterize "racism"; be that as it may, it defines "racial segregation". As indicated by the 1965 UN International Convention on the Elimination of All Forms of Racial Discrimination,

The expression "racial separation" will mean any qualification, avoidance, limitation. Or inclination dependent on race, shading, plunge, or national or ethnic root that has the reason or impact of invalidating or impeding the acknowledgement, happiness or exercise, on an equal balance, of human rights and critical opportunities in the political, financial, social, social or some other field of open life.

In their 1978 UNESCO Declaration on Race and Racial Prejudice, the UN expresses, "Every individual have a place with a single animal type and are slipped from a typical stock. They are brought into the world equivalent in respect and rights and all structure a vital piece of humanity."

The UN meaning of racial separation doesn't make any differentiation between segregation dependent on ethnicity and race, to some degree because the qualification between the two has involved a discussion among scholastics, including anthropologists. Also, in British law, the racial expression gathering signifies "any gathering of individuals who are characterized by reference to their race, shading, nationality (counting citizenship) or ethnic or national cause".

In Norway, "race" has been expelled from national laws concerning segregation because the utilization of the expression is viewed as hazardous and untrustworthy. The Norwegian Anti-Discrimination Act bans separation dependent on ethnicity, national starting point, plummet, and skin shading.

Social and conduct sciences

Sociologists, as a rule, perceive "race" as social development. This implies, although the ideas of race and racism depend on perceptible organic attributes, any ends drawn about race based on those perceptions are vigorously impacted by social philosophies. Racism, as a philosophy, exists in the general public at both the individual and institutional level.

While a significant part of the examination and work on racism during the last 50 years or so has focused on "white racism" in the Western world, verifiable records of race-based social practices can be found over the globe. In this manner, racism can be extensively characterized to envelop individual and gathering preferences and demonstrations of separation that bring about material and social points of interest presented on a more significant part of a predominant social gathering. Purported "white racism" centers around social orders in which white populaces are the lion's share or the dominant social group. In investigations of these dominant part white social orders, the total of material and favorable social circumstances is usually named "white benefit".

Race and race relations are noticeable regions of study in humanism and financial aspects—a significant part of the sociological writing centers around white racism. Probably the most punctual sociological deals with racism were written by humanist W. E. B. Du Bois, the leading African American to acquire a doctoral qualification from Harvard University. Du Bois expressed, "[t]he issue of the twentieth century is the issue of the shading line." Wellman (1993) characterizes racism as "socially endorsed convictions, which, paying little heed to expectations included, guard the favorable circumstances whites have due to the subjected position of racial minorities". In both humanism and financial matters, the results of supremacist activities are regularly estimated by the disparity in salary, riches, total assets, and access to other social assets, (for example, training), between racial gatherings.

In humanism and social brain research, racial character and the securing of that personality is frequently utilized as a variable in racism considers. Racial philosophies and racial character influence people's impression of race and separation. Cazenave and Maddern (1999) characterize racism as "an exceptionally composed arrangement of 'race'- based gathering benefit that works at each degree of society and is held together by a complex philosophy of shading/'race' matchless quality. Racial centrality (the degree to which a culture perceives people's racial character) seems to influence the level of segregation African American youthful grown-ups to see. However, racial philosophy may cushion the impeding enthusiastic impacts of that separation." Sellers and Shelton (2003) found that a connection between racial segregation and passionate misery was directed by racial philosophy and social convictions.

A few sociologists additionally contend that, especially in the West, where racism is regularly contrarily authorized in the public arena. Racism has changed from being unmitigated to an increasingly clandestine articulation of racial preference. The "more current" (frequently covered up and less effectively discernible) types of racism – which can be viewed as implanted in standard procedures and structures – are progressively hard to investigate just as a challenge. It has been proposed that, while in numerous nations clear or explicit racism has gotten no-no progressively. Even among the individuals who show libertarian express perspectives, verifiable or aversive racism is as yet looked after subliminally.

This procedure has been concentrated broadly in social brain science as specific affiliations and verifiable mentalities, a segment of understood insight. Understood attitudes are assessments that happen without conscious mindfulness towards a disposition object or oneself. These assessments are commonly either positive or ominous. They occur from different impacts in the individual experience. Verifiable mentalities are not intentionally recognized (or they are erroneously distinguished) hints of experience that intercede positive or troublesome sentiments, contemplations, or activities towards social items. These emotions, reflections, or actions affect the conduct of which the individual may not know.

Consequently, subliminal racism can impact our visual handling and how our brains work when we are subconsciously presented to countenances of various hues. In pondering wrongdoing, for instance, social analyst Jennifer L. Eberhardt (2004) of Stanford University holds that "darkness is so connected with wrongdoing you're prepared to select these wrongdoing objects." Such exposures impact our psyches, and they can cause subliminal racism in our conduct towards others or even towards objects. In this way, supremacist musings and activities can emerge from generalizations and fears of which we don't know.

Humanities

Language, semantics, and talk are dynamic zones of study in the humanities, alongside writing and expressions of the human experience. Talk investigation tries to uncover the importance of race and the activities of racists through careful examination of the manners by which these variables of human culture are depicted and examined in different composed and oral works. For instance, Van Dijk (1992) looks at the changed manners by which portrayals of racism and supremacist activities are delineated by the culprits of such events just as by their casualties. He noticed that when depictions of activities have negative ramifications for the lion's share, and particularly for white elites, they are frequently observed as disputable and such dubious translations are regularly set apart with quotes. Or they are welcomed with articulations of separation or uncertainty— the recently referred to the book, The Souls of Black Folk by WEB. Du Bois, speaks to early African-American writing that depicts the writer's encounters with racism when he was going in the South as an African American.

Much American anecdotal writing has concentrated on issues of racism and the dark "racial experience" in the US, including works composed by whites, for example, Uncle Tom's Cabin, To Kill a Mockingbird, and Imitation of Life, or even the true to life work Black Like Me. These books feed into what has been known as the "white friend in need account in the film", in which the saints and courageous women are white although the story is about things that happen to dark characters. Printed investigation of such works can balance forcefully with dark creators' depictions of African Americans and their encounters in US society. African American scholars have some of the time been depicted in African-American examinations as withdrawing from racial issues when they expound on "whiteness". In contrast, others recognize this as an African American artistic custom called "the writing of white offence", some portion of a multi-pronged exertion to challenge and destroy racial domination in the US.

Mainstream use and types of racism

As indicated by word references, the word is ordinarily used to depict preference and segregation dependent on race. Racism can likewise be said to represent a condition in the public arena where a prevailing racial gathering profit by the abuse of others, regardless of whether that gathering needs such advantages or not. Foucauldian researcher Ladelle McWhorter, in her 2009 book, Racism and Sexual Oppression in Anglo-America. A Genealogy, sets present-day racism also, concentrating on the idea of a predominant gathering, usually whites, competing for racial immaculateness and progress, as opposed to a clear or evident philosophy focused on the abuse of nonwhites.

Infamous use, as in some academic utilization, little qualification is made among "racism" and "ethnocentrism". Regularly, the two are recorded together as "racial and ethnic" in depicting some activity or result that is related with preference inside a more significant part or regular gathering in the public eye. Moreover, the importance of the term racism is frequently conflated with the terms partiality, fanaticism, and segregation. Racism is an unpredictable idea that can include each of those; yet it can't be likened with, nor is it equivalent, with these different terms.

The term is regularly utilized according to what is viewed as bias inside a minority or enslaved gathering, as in the idea of reverse racism. "Turn around racism" is an idea frequently used to portray demonstrations of segregation or threatening vibe against individuals from a predominant racial or ethnic gathering while at the same time preferring individuals from minority gatherings. This idea has been utilized mainly in the United States in banters over cognizant shading arrangements, (for example, governmental policy regarding minorities in society) expected to cure racial disparities. Those[who?] who battle for the interests of ethnic minorities regularly dismiss the idea of reverse racism. Researchers additionally usually characterize racism as far as individual preference, yet additionally as far as a force structure that ensures the interests of the dominant society and effectively oppresses ethnic minorities. From this point of view, while individuals from ethnic minorities might be biased against individuals from the dominant culture, they come up short on the political and monetary capacity to abuse them forcefully, and they are along these lines not rehearsing "racism".

Aversive racism

Aversive racism is a type of correct racism, wherein an individual's oblivious negative assessments of racial or ethnic minorities are acknowledged by a steady evasion of cooperation with other racial and ethnic gatherings. Instead of customary, unmistakable racism, which is portrayed by apparent disdain for and unequivocal victimization racial/ethnic minorities. Aversive racism is described by progressively intricate, undecided articulations and mentalities. Aversive racism is comparative in suggestions to the idea of a representative or present-day racism, which is likewise a type of individual, oblivious, or clandestine mentality which brings about unconscious types of separation.

The term was begotten by Joel Kovel to portray the unpretentious racial practices of any ethnic or racial gathering who defend their antipathy for a specific group by the claim to rules or generalizations. Individuals who carry on in an aversively racial manner may pronounce libertarian convictions. And will frequently deny their racially persuaded conduct; all things considered, they change their behaviour when managing an individual from another race or ethnic gathering than the one they have a place with. The inspiration for the change is believed to be understood or subliminal. Analyses have offered experimental help for the presence of aversive racism. Aversive racism has been appeared to have possibly positive ramifications for dynamic in work, in legitimate choices and in helping conduct.

Visual impairment

Corresponding to racism, partial blindness is the dismissal of racial attributes in social communication, for instance in the release of governmental policy regarding minorities in society, as an approach to address the aftereffects of past examples of segregation. Pundits of this mentality contend that by declining to take care of racial aberrations, racial visual impairment in actuality unwittingly sustains the models that produce racial imbalance.

Eduardo Bonilla-Silva contends that visually challenged racism emerges from "theoretical progressivism, neologism of culture, naturalization of racial issues, and minimization of racism". Partially blind practices are "inconspicuous, institutional, and nonracial" because race is unequivocally disregarded in dynamic. If competition is ignored in overwhelmingly white populaces, for instance, whiteness turns into the standardizing standard. However, non-white individuals are othered, and the racism these people experience might be limited or deleted. At an individual level, individuals with "visually challenged partiality" dismiss supremacist belief system, yet besides, deny fundamental strategies proposed to fix institutional racism.

Social

Social racism shows as cultural convictions and customs that advance the presumption that the results of a given culture, including the language and conventions of that culture, are better than those of different societies. It imparts a lot to xenophobia, which is frequently described by the dread of, or hatred toward, individuals from an outgroup by individuals from an ingroup. In that sense, it is additionally like communalism as utilized in South Asia.

Social racism exists when there is an across the board acknowledgement of generalizations concerning diverse ethnic or populace gatherings. Though the conviction can describe racism that one race is intrinsically better than another, social racism can be portrayed by the belief that one culture is characteristically better than another.

Monetary

Chronicled financial or social difference is asserted to be a type of segregation brought about by past racism and valid reasons, influencing the current age through shortages in the proper instruction and sorts of arrangement in previous generations, and through principally oblivious supremacist mentalities and activities on individuals from everyone. In 2011, Bank of America consented to pay $335 million to settle a government guarantee that it is home loan division, Countrywide Financial, victimized dark and Hispanic homebuyers.

During the Spanish pilgrim time frame, Spaniards built up an intricate standing framework dependent on race, which was utilized for social control, and which likewise decided an individual's significance in the public eye. While numerous Latin American nations had since a long time, ago rendered the framework formally illicit through enactment, typically at the hour of their autonomy, bias dependent on degrees of saw good racial ways from European heritage joined with one's financial status stay, a repercussion of the frontier position framework.

Institutional

Institutional racism (otherwise called auxiliary racism, state racism or foundational racism) is racial segregation by governments, companies, religions, or instructive establishments or other huge associations with the ability to impact the lives of numerous people. Stokely Carmichael is credited for authoring the expression of institutional racism in the late 1960s. He characterized the term as "the aggregate disappointment of an association to give proper and expert support of individuals in light of their shading, culture or ethnic source".

Maulana Karenga contended that racism established the pulverization of culture, language, religion, and human chance and that the impacts of racism were "the ethically tremendous annihilation of human chance included reclassifying African humankind to the world, harming past, present and future relations with other people who just know us through this generalizing and consequently harming the genuinely human relations among people groups".

Othering

Othering is the term utilized by some to portray an arrangement of segregation whereby the attributes of a gathering are used to recognize them as discrete from the standard. Othering assumes a vital job in the history and continuation of racism. To typify a culture as something other than what's expected, colorful or immature is, to sum up, that it doesn't care for 'ordinary' society. Europe's pilgrim demeanor towards the Orientals epitomizes this as it was felt that the East was something contrary to the West; female where the West was manly, frail where the West was stable and customary where the West was dynamic. By making these speculations and othering the East, Europe was at the same time characterizing herself as the standard, further digging in the hole.

A significant part of the procedure of othering depends on the envisioned distinction or the desire for contrast. Spatial contrast can be sufficient to reason that "we" are "here" and the "others" are over "there". Envisioned variations serve to classify individuals into gatherings, and dole out them attributes that suit the imaginer's desires.

Racial separation

Racial separation is any victimization people based on their skin shading or racial or ethnic root. People can separate by declining to work with, associate with, or share assets with individuals of a specific gathering. Governments can separate acceptably or expressly in law, for instance through approaches of racial isolation, a unique requirement of rules, or lopsided allotment of assets. A few wards have hostile to separation laws which restrict the administration or people from segregating dependent on race (and in some cases different components) in different conditions. A few foundations and rules utilize governmental policy regarding minorities in society to endeavor to survive or make up for the impacts of racial separation. Now and again, this is a substantially improved enrollment of individuals from underrepresented gatherings; in different cases, there are rigid racial standards. Adversaries of reliable cures like quantities describe them as opposite segregation, where individuals from a predominant or more magnificent part bunch are oppressed.

Limit issues and related types of segregation

Racial limits can include a wide range of components, (for example, family, physical appearance, national birthplace, language, religion, and culture), and possibly set in law by governments, or may rely upon nearby social standards.

Segregation dependent on skin color,(measured for instance on the Fitzpatrick scale) is firmly identified with racial separation, as skin shading is frequently utilized as an intermediary for a race in ordinary associations, and is one factor used by lawful frameworks that apply point by point standards. For instance, the Population Registration Act, 1950 was utilized to implement the politically-sanctioned racial segregation framework in South Africa, and also, Brazil has set up sheets to dole out a racial class to individuals to authorize racial amounts. In light of hereditary variety, skin shading and other physical appearance can fluctuate impressively even among kin. Others recognize a few kids with similar guardians either self-distinguish or as being of various races. At times, the same individual is known as an alternate race on a birth authentication versus a demise testament. Various principles, (for example, hypodescent versus hyperdescent) order similar individuals in an unexpected way, and for different reasons, a few people "go" as an individual from a surprising race in comparison to they would be some way or another be grouped in, conceivably evading legal or relational segregation.

A given race is some of the time characterized as a lot of ethnicities from populaces in neighboring geographic territories, (for example, a landmass like Australia or a subcontinental locale like South Asia) that are commonly comparable in appearance. In such cases, racial segregation can happen because somebody is of an ethnicity characterized as outside that race, or ethnic separation (or ethnic scorn, ethnic clash, and ethnic brutality) can occur between bunches who consider each other to be a similar race. Segregation dependent on rank is comparative; since the station is genetic, individuals of the same standing are generally viewed as of a similar race and ethnicity.

An individual's national root (the nation wherein they were conceived or have citizenship) is now and again utilized in deciding an individual's ethnicity or race. However, separation dependent on national inception can likewise be free of the race (and is once in a while explicitly tended to in hostile to segregation laws). Language and culture are once in a while markers of national birthplace and can incite occurrences of separation depends on the national starting point. For instance, somebody of a South Asian ethnicity who experienced childhood in London, speaks British English with a London highlight, and whose family has absorbed to British culture may be dealt with better than somebody of a similar ethnicity who is an ongoing migrant and speaks Indian English. Such a distinction in treatment may in any case casually be depicted as a type of racism, or all the more absolutely as xenophobia or against foreigner feeling.

In nations where relocation, unification, or separation has happened moderately as of late, the procedure of ethnogenesis may confuse the assurance of both ethnicity and race and is identified with individual personality or connection. Some of the time, the ethnicity of foreigners in their new nation is characterized as their national starting point, and length various races. For instance, the 2015 Community Survey of the United States Census acknowledged distinguishing proof as Mexican Americans of any race (for example including Native Americans from Mexico, relatives of Africans shipped to New Spain as subjugated individuals, and relatives of Spanish settlers). In studies taken by the Mexican government, similar individuals would have been depicted as indigenous, dark, or white (with an enormous number of individuals unclassified who may be portrayed as Mestizo). The US enumeration poses separate inquiries about Hispanic and Latino Americans to recognize language from racial personality. Segregation dependent on being Hispanic or Latino occurs in the United States. It may be viewed as a type of racial separation if "Hispanic" or "Latino" are seen as another racial classification got from ethnicities which shaped after the freedom of the former provinces of the Americas. Numerous factual reports apply the two qualities, for instance, contrasting Non-Hispanic whites with different gatherings.

At the point when individuals of various races are dealt with quickly, choices about how to treat a specific individual raise the question of which racial characterization that individual has a place with. For instance, meanings of whiteness in the United States were utilized before the social equality development with the end goal of migration and the capacity to hold citizenship or be oppressed. On the off chance that a race is characterized as a lot of ethnolinguistic gatherings, at that point, the primary language starting point can be utilized to describe the limits of that gathering. The status of Finns as white was tested because the Finnish language is Uralic instead of Indo-European, purportedly making the Finns of the Mongoloid race. The essential American ideal that all individuals of topographically European family and fair complexion are "white" won for Finns and other European workers like Irish Americans and Italian Americans whose whiteness was tested and who confronted relational if not legal segregation. American and South African laws which separated the populace into whites from Europe and blacks from sub-Saharan Africa frequently caused issues of translation when managing individuals from different territories, for example, the remainder of the Mediterranean Basin, Asia, North Africa, or even Native Americans, with the order as non-white ordinarily bringing about legal segregation. (Some Native American clans have bargain rights which award benefits as opposed to drawbacks. However, these were frequently haggled on negative standing.) Though as an ethnic-strict gathering they regularly face strict segregation, the whiteness of all Jews was likewise tested in the United States, with endeavors to order them as Asiatic (Palestine being in western Asia) or Semitic (which would also incorporate Arabs). The whole family line of most Jewish individuals is more changed than primarily old Hebrew clans. As the Jewish diaspora spread across Europe and Africa after some time, numerous Jewish ethnic divisions emerged, bringing about Jews who distinguish as white, dark, and different races. The reunification of various populaces in current Israel has prompted a few issues of racial oppression more mysterious-looking Jews by fair looking Jews.

By and large patterns

A 2013 investigation of World Values Survey information by The Washington Post took a gander at the portion of individuals in every nation that showed they would lean toward not to have neighbors of a similar race. It extended from beneath 5% in Australia, New Zealand, and numerous nations in the Americas, to 51.4% in Jordan; Europe had a wide variety, from underneath

5% in the UK, Norway, and Sweden, to 22.7% in France. Over 30 years of field exploratory examinations have discovered noteworthy degrees of oppression non-whites in labor, lodging, and item showcases in 10 unique nations.

The Netherlands
An investigation led in the Netherlands and distributed in 2013 discovered vast degrees of victimization work candidates with Arabic-sounding names.

Africa
The British pioneer sway enormously influenced the way of life of African culture; however, the distinctions in the nations like Nigeria stay as near convention contrasted with countries like South Africa. American racism additionally has an impact that heightens racism in Nigeria; however, American racism thoughts affecting African Cultures. The racism that was created by the effects of colonization and American affected there to make levels of intensity-dependent on racism. Racism in African societies are associated with the open doors got throughout everyday life, infection helplessness, and old conventions. For instance, in the north, a backhanded arrangement of rule settled another lifestyle between the colonizing government and the Fulani-Hausa administering class. Due to this, the North falls behind the South and West on instruction advancement, which causes racial harm.

Racism in the human services framework

Racial predisposition exists in the clinical field influencing how patients are dealt with and how they are analyzed. There are cases where patients' words are not paid attention to; a model would be the ongoing case with Serena Williams. After the introduction of her little girl employing C-segment, the tennis player started to feel torment and brevity of breath. It took her multiple times to persuade the attendant they paid attention to her self-said manifestations. Had she not been relentless and requested a CT check, which indicated coagulation bringing about blood diminishing, Williams may not have been alive. This is only one of many situations where fundamental racism can influence ladies of shading in pregnancy entanglements.

One of the variables that lead to higher death rates among dark moms is the ineffectively adapted emergency clinics and absence of standard human services offices. Alongside having conveyances done in immature territories, circumstance becomes confused when the torment managed by patients are not paid attention to by social insurance suppliers. Suffering got notification from patients of shading are thought little of by specialists contrasted with misery told by patients who are white driving them to misdiagnose.

Many states that the instruction level of individuals influence whether they admit to human services offices, inclining to the contention that non-white individuals intentionally maintain a strategic distance from emergency clinics contrasted with white partners notwithstanding, this isn't the situation. Indeed, even Serena Williams, a notable competitor, was not paid attention to when she depicted her torment. The facts demonstrate that the encounters of patients in emergency clinic settings impact whether they come back to medicinal services offices. Dark individuals are less inclined to admit to clinics anyway those that are conceded have longer remains than white individuals.

The more extended hospitalization of dark patients doesn't improve care conditions, it aggravates it, particularly when rewarded ineffectively by personnel. Not a ton of minorities is conceded into medical clinics and those that are getting poor adapted treatment and care. This segregation results in misdiagnosis and clinical slip-ups that lead to high passing rates.

Although the Medicaid program was passed to guarantee African Americans and different minorities got the social insurance treatment they merited and to confine separation in clinic offices, there still is by all accounts a primary reason for the low number of dark patients admitted to emergency clinics, as not getting the best possible measurement of prescription. New child death rates and futures of minorities are a lot of lower than that of white individuals in the United States. Sicknesses like malignancy and heart maladies are progressively common in minorities, which is one of the components for the high death rate in the gathering. Anyway are not rewarded as needs are.

Although projects like Medicaid exist to help minorities, there still is, by all accounts, an enormous number of individuals who are not guaranteed. This budgetary downside demoralizes individuals in the gathering to go to medical clinics and specialists workplaces.

Financial and social impacts can affect how patients are treated by their medicinal services suppliers. At the point when specialists incline a patient, it can prompt the development of generalizations, changing how they see their patient's information and conclusion, influencing the treatment plan they actualize.

Turn around segregation

Turn around segregation is a term for charges that the individual from a predominant or dominant part bunch has languished separation over the advantage of a minority or verifiably burdened gathering.

US

In the United States, courts have maintained race-cognizant approaches when they are utilized to advance a different work or instructive condition. A few pundits have depicted those approaches as victimizing white individuals. In light of contentions that such methods (for example governmental policy regarding minorities in society) comprise victimization whites, sociologists note that the reason for these arrangements is to even the odds to check segregation.

Discernments

A 2016 survey found that 38% of US residents imagined that Whites confronted a ton of separation. Among Democrats, 29% idea there was some oppression Whites in the United States, while 49% of Republicans thought the equivalent. Likewise, another survey led prior in the year found that 41% of US residents accepted there were "boundless" oppression whites. There is proof that a few people are spurred to admit they are the survivors of opposite separation because the conviction reinforces their confidence.

Law

In the US, Act-VII of the Civil Rights Act of 1964 precludes all racial separation dependent on race. Albeit a few courts have taken the position that a white individual must satisfy an uplifted guideline of evidence to demonstrate a converse separation guarantee, the US Equivalent Employment Opportunity Commission (EEOC) applies a similar standard to all cases of racial separation regardless of the casualty's race.

Racial isolation

Racial isolation is the detachment of people into socially-developed racial gatherings in everyday life. It might apply to exercises, for example, eating in an eatery, drinking from a drinking fountain, utilizing a restroom, going to class, going out to see the films, or in the rental or acquisition of a home. Isolation is commonly prohibited, yet may exist through accepted practices, in any event, when there is no strong individual inclination for it, as recommended by Thomas Schelling's models of isolation and ensuing work.

Supremacy

Racial oppressor mentalities frequently defended hundreds of years of European expansionism in the Americas, Africa and Asia. During the mid-twentieth century, the expression "The White Man's Burden" was broadly used to legitimize a colonialist approach as an essential undertaking. A hobby for the arrangement of triumph and oppression of Native Americans radiated from the generalized impression of the indigenous individuals as "coldblooded Indian savages" (as depicted in the United States Declaration of Independence). In an 1890 article about provincial extension onto Native American land, writer L. Straight to the point Baum expressed: "The Whites, by the law of triumph, by the equity of development, are experts of the American landmass, and the best wellbeing of the outskirts settlements will be made sure about by the complete demolition of the scarcely any outstanding Indians." Attitudes of dark matchless quality, Arab incomparability, and East Asian incomparable quality likewise exist.

Representative/current

A few researchers contend that in the US, prior brutal and forceful types of racism have advanced into an increasingly unpretentious kind of bias in the late twentieth century. This new type of racism is now and then alluded to as "current racism", and it is described by ostensibly acting impartial while internally keeping up biased perspectives, showing unobtrusive partial practices, for example, activities educated by ascribing characteristics to others dependent on racial generalizations, and assessing similar conduct diversely reliant on the race of the individual being assessed. This view depends on investigations of bias and oppressive conduct, where a few people will act irresolutely towards dark individuals, with constructive responses in specific, progressively open settings, however increasingly contrary perspectives and articulations in progressively private settings. This inner conflict may likewise be apparent, for instance, in recruiting choices where occupation competitors that are in any case decidedly assessed might be unwittingly disfavored by bosses in an official conclusion in light of their race. A few researchers believe current racism to be described by a definite dismissal of generalizations, joined with protection from changing structures of segregation for reasons that are nonracial, a belief system that considers opportunity at an only singular premise precluding the importance from securing race in deciding only chances and the show of roundabout types of smaller scale hostility toward as well as evasion of individuals of different sports.

Subliminal inclinations

Ongoing exploration has indicated that people who intentionally guarantee to dismiss racism may even now show race-based inner mind inclinations in their effective procedures. While such "subliminal racial inclinations" don't completely fit the meaning of racism, their effect can be comparative, however normally less articulated, not being express, conscious or intentional.

Universal law and racial separation

In 1919, a proposition to incorporate a racial correspondence arrangement in the Covenant of the League of Nations was bolstered by a more significant part, however not received in the Paris Peace Conference in 1919. In 1943, Japan and its partners announced work for the cancellation of racial segregation to be their focus on the Greater East Asia Conference. Article 1 of the 1945 UN Charter incorporates "advancing and empowering regard for human rights and crucial opportunities for all without qualification as to race" as UN reason.

In 1950, UNESCO recommended in The Race Question – an announcement marked by 21 researchers, for example, Ashley Montagu, Claude Lévi-Strauss, Gunnar Myrdal, Julian Huxley, and so forth – to "drop the term race by and large and rather discuss ethnic gatherings". The announcement denounced logical racism speculations that had assumed a job in the Holocaust. It pointed both at exposing valid supremacist speculations, by promoting present-day information concerning "the race question", and ethically sentenced racism as despite the way of thinking of the Enlightenment and its suspicion of equivalent rights for all. Alongside Myrdal's An American Dilemma: The Negro Problem and Modern Democracy (1944), The Race Question impacted the 1954 US Incomparable Court integration choice in "Earthy coloured v. Leading group of

Education." Also, in 1950, the European Convention was embraced, which was generally utilized on racial separation issues.

The United Nations utilize the meaning of racial segregation spread out in the International Convention on Racial Discrimination, embraced in 1966:

... any qualification, prohibition, limitation or inclination dependent on race, shading, plummet, or national or ethnic source that has the reason or impact of invalidating or debilitating the acknowledgement, pleasure or exercise, on an equal balance, of human rights and critical opportunities in the political, financial, social, social or some other field of open life. (Section 1 of Article 1 of the UN Universal Convention on the Elimination of All Forms of Racial Discrimination)

In 2001, the European Union expressly restricted racism, alongside numerous different types of social segregation, in the Charter of Fundamental Human Rights of the European Union, the lawful impact of which, assuming any, would necessarily be constrained to Institutions of the European Union: "Article 21 of the sanction precludes separation on any ground, for example, race, shading, ethnic or social root, hereditary highlights, language, religion or conviction, political or some other sentiment, the participation of a national minority, property, handicap, age or sexual direction and separation on the grounds of nationality."

Belief system

Racism existed during the nineteenth century as "logical racism", which endeavored to give a racial order of humankind. In 1775 Johann Blumenbach partitioned the total populace into five gatherings as indicated by skin shading (Caucasians, Mongols, and so forth.), setting the view that the non-Caucasians had emerged through a procedure of degeneration. Another new view in logical racism was the polygenist see, which held that the various races had been independently made. Polygenist Christoph Meiners, for instance, split humankind into two divisions which he named the "excellent White race" and the "revolting Black race". In his book, The Outline of History of Mankind, he asserted that a principle standard for the race is either excellence or grotesqueness. He saw just the white race as incredible. He believed appalling breeds to be mediocre, shameless and creature-like.

Anders Retzius exhibited that neither Europeans nor others are one "unadulterated race", yet of blended inceptions. While defamed, determinations of Blumenbach's scientific categorization are still broadly utilized for the order of the populace in the United States. Hans Peder Steensby, while unequivocally underlining that all people today are of blended starting points, in 1907 asserted that the roots of social contrasts must be followed uncommonly far back in time, and guessed that the "most flawless race" today would be the Australian Aboriginals.

Logical racism becomes emphatically undesirable in the mid-twentieth century, however, the causes of fundamental human and cultural contrasts are still looked into the inside scholarly community, in fields, for example, human hereditary qualities including paleogenetics, human social studies, similar governmental issues, history of religions, history of thoughts, ancient times, history, morals, and psychiatry. There is across the board dismissal of any procedure dependent on anything like Blumenbach's races. It is progressively hazy to which degree and when ethnic and national generalizations are acknowledged.

Albeit after World War II and the Holocaust, bigot belief systems were undermined on moral, political and logical grounds, racism and racial separation have stayed across the board far and wide.

Du Bois saw that it isn't so much "race" that we consider, yet culture: "... a typical history, natural laws and religion, comparable propensities for thought and a conscious endeavoring together for specific beliefs of life". Late nineteenth-century patriots were the first to grasp contemporary talks on "race", ethnicity, and "natural selection" to shape new patriot principles. At last, the race came to speak to not just the most significant characteristics of the human body, but on the other hand, was viewed as conclusively moulding the character and character of the country. As per this view, culture is the physical sign made by ethnic groupings, as such, entirely controlled by racial attributes. Religion and race became considered interwoven and ward upon one another, occasionally even to the degree of including nationality or language to the arrangement of definition. Immaculateness of the race would, in general, be identified with rather shallow qualities that were expertly tended to and publicized, for example, blondness. Racial characteristics would, in general, be determined with nationality and language as opposed to the natural geographic circulation of racial qualities. On account of Nordicism, the section "Germanic" was identical to the predominance of race.

Supported by some patriot and ethnocentric qualities and accomplishments of decision, this idea of racial prevalence developed over recognize from different societies that were viewed as substandard or debased. This accentuation on culture compares to the cutting edge standard meaning of racism: "racism doesn't begin from the presence of 'races'. It makes them through a procedure of social division into classifications: anyone can be racialised, freely of their substantial, social, strict contrasts."

This definition expressly overlooks the fundamental idea of race, which is as yet dependent upon logical discussion. In the expressions of David C. Rowe, "racial idea, albeit at times in the presence of another name, will stay being used in science and different fields since researchers, just as laypeople, are entranced by assorted human variety, some of which is caught by race."

Ethnicity and ethnic clashes

Discussions over the beginnings of racism regularly experience the ill effects of an absence of clarity over the term. Many utilize the expression "racism" to allude to increasingly broad wonders, for example, xenophobia and ethnocentrism, even though researchers endeavor to unmistakably recognize those marvels from racism as a belief system or from logical racism, which has little to do with customary xenophobia. Others conflate ongoing types of racism with previous examples of an ethnic and national clash. By and large, ethnonational encounter appears to owe itself to struggle over land and vital assets. At times, ethnicity and patriotism were bridled all together to mobilize soldiers in wars between extraordinary strict domains (for instance, the Muslim Turks and the Catholic Austro-Hungarians).

Ideas of different races and racism have frequently assumed focal jobs in ethnic clashes. From the beginning of time, when an enemy is recognized as "other" because of ideas of race or ethnicity (specifically when "other" is deciphered to signify "mediocre"), the methods utilized by oneself assumed "prevalent" gathering to a fitting area, human asset, or material riches frequently have been increasingly merciless, progressively ruthless, and less compelled by ethical or moral contemplations.

As indicated by antiquarian Daniel Richter, Pontiac's Rebellion saw the rise on the two sides of the contention of "the clever thought that every single Native individual were 'Indians,' that all Euro-Americans were 'Whites,' and that all must join in devastating the other". Basil Davidson states in his narrative, Africa: Different however Equal, that racism, truth be told, just barely as of late surfaced as late as the nineteenth century, because of the requirement for a legitimization for subjugation in the Americas.

Generally, racism was a significant main thrust behind the Transatlantic slave exchange. It was additionally a substantial power behind racial isolation, particularly in the United States in the nineteenth and mid-twentieth hundreds of years, and South Africa under politically-sanctioned racial segregation; nineteenth and twentieth-century racism in the Western world is exceptionally all around archived and comprises a reference point in studies and talks about racism. Racism has assumed a job in massacres, for example, the Armenian slaughter, and the Holocaust, and pilgrim ventures like the European colonization of the Americas, Africa, and Asia. Indigenous people groups have been – and are – frequently dependent upon bigot perspectives. The United Nations denounces practices and belief systems of racism in the Declaration of Human Rights.

Ethnic and racial patriotism

After the Napoleonic Wars, Europe was stood up to with the new "nationalities question", prompting reconfigurations of the European guide, on which the outskirts between the states had been depicted during the 1648 Peace of Westphalia. Patriotism had shown up with the creation of the levée as a group by the French Revolutionaries, in this manner imagining mass enrollment to have the option to safeguard the recently established Republic against the Ancien Régime request spoke to by the European governments. This prompted the French Revolutionary Wars (1792–1802) and afterwards to the victories of Napoleon, and to the ensuing European-wide discussions on the ideas and real factors of countries, and specifically of country states. The Westphalia Treaty had isolated Europe into different domains and realms, (for example, the Ottoman Empire, the Holy Roman, the Swedish Empire, the Kingdom of France, and so forth.), and for a considerable length of time wars were pursued between sovereigns (Kabinettskriege in German).

Current country states showed up in the wake of the French Revolution, with the development of enthusiastic suppositions without precedent for Spain during the Peninsula War (1808–1813, referred to in Spain as the Independence War). Despite the rebuilding of the past request with the 1815 Congress of Vienna, the "nationalities question" turned into the principle issue of Europe during the Industrial Era, driving species to the 1848 Revolutions, the Italian unification finished during the 1871

Franco-Prussian War, which itself ended in the decree of the German in the Hall of Mirrors in the Palace of Versailles, subsequently accomplishing the German unification.

In the interim, the Ottoman Empire, the "debilitated man of Europe", was gone up against with continuous patriot developments, which, alongside the dissolving of the Austrian-Hungarian Empire, would prompt the creation, after World War I, of the different country conditions of the Balkans, with "national minorities" in their outskirts.

Ethnic patriotism, which upheld the faith in a genetic enrollment of the country, showed up in the recorded setting encompassing the production of the cutting edge country states.

One of its primary impacts was the Romantic patriot development at the turn of the nineteenth century, spoke to by figures, for example, Johann Herder (1744–1803), Johan Fichte in the Addresses to the German Nation (1808), Friedrich Hegel, or additionally, in France, Jules Michelet (1798–1874). It was against liberal patriotism, spoke to by creators, for example, Ernest Renan (1823–1892), who considered the country as a network, which, rather than being founded on the Volk ethnic gathering and a particular, primary language, was established on the abstract will to live respectively ("the country is an everyday plebiscite", 1882) or likewise John Stuart Mill (1806–1873). Ethnic patriotism mixed with logical bigot talks, just as with "mainland radical" (Hannah Arendt, 1951) talks, for instance in the dish Germanism talks, which hypothesized the racial predominance of the German Volk (individuals/society). The Pan-German League (Alldeutscher Verband), made in 1891, advanced German colonialism and "racial cleanliness", and was against intermarriage with Jews. Another mainstream current, the Völkisch development, was likewise a significant defender of the German ethnic patriot talk, and it joined Pan-Germanism with present-day racial discrimination against Jews. Individuals from the Völkisch event, specifically the Thule Society, would take an interest in the establishing of the German Workers' Party (DAP) in Munich in 1918, the antecedent of the National Socialist German Workers' Party (NSDAP; ordinarily referred to in English as the Nazi party). Dish Germanism assumed a conclusive job in the interwar time of the 1920s–1930s.

These flows started to relate the possibility of the country with the original idea of an "ace race" (regularly the "Aryan race" or the "Nordic race") gave from the logical bigot talk. They conflated nationalities with ethnic gatherings, called "races", in an extreme qualification from past racial discussions that set the presence of a "race battle" inside the country and the state itself. Moreover, they accepted that political limits should reflect these supposed racial and ethnic gatherings, in this manner advocating ethnic purifying, to accomplish "racial virtue" and to accomplish ethnic homogeneity in the country state.

Such bigot talks joined with patriotism, were not, nonetheless, constrained to skillet Germanism. In France, the progress from liberal Republican nationalism, to ethnic patriotism, which made patriotism a quality of far-right developments in France, occurred during the Dreyfus Affair toward the finish of the nineteenth century. During quite a while, and across the nation emergency influenced French society, concerning the supposed injustice of Alfred Dreyfus, a French Jewish military official. The nation captivated itself into two inverse camps, one spoke to by Émile Zola, who composed J'Accuse... ! with regards to Alfred Dreyfus, and the other spoke to by the patriot writer, Maurice Barrès (1862–1923), one of the organizers of the ethnic patriot talk in France. Simultaneously, Charles Maurras (1868–1952), author of the monarchist Action française development, speculated the "counter France", made out of the "four confederate conditions of Protestants, Jews, Freemasons and outsiders" (his real word for the last being the disparaging métèques). For sure, to him, the initial three were all "inside outsiders", who compromised the ethnic solidarity of the French individuals.

History Of racism

Ethnocentrism and proto-racism

Bernard Lewis has referred to the Greek logician Aristotle who, in his conversation of subjugation, expressed that while Greeks are free commonly, "brutes" (non-Greeks) are slaves naturally, in that it is in their inclination to be all the more ready to submit to a tyrannical government. Although Aristotle doesn't determine a specific race, he contends that individuals from countries outside Greece are more inclined to the weight of servitude than those from Greece. While Aristotle offers comments about the most common slaves being those with robust bodies and slave spirits (unfit for the rule, unintelligent) which would appear to suggest a real reason for segregation, he likewise expressly expresses that the correct sort of minds and bodies don't generally go together, inferring that the best determinate for mediocrity and regular slaves versus ordinary experts in the spirit, not the body. This proto-racism is viewed as a significant forerunner to present-day racism by classicist Benjamin Isaac.

Such proto-racism and ethnocentrism must be taken a gander at inside setting because a cutting edge comprehension of racism dependent on inherited mediocrity (with present-day racism dependent on selective breeding and logical racism) was not yet evolved. It is indistinct whether Aristotle accepted the common inadequacy of Barbarians was brought about by condition and atmosphere (in the same way as other of his counterparts) or by birth. Student of history Dante A. Puzzo, in his conversation of Aristotle, racism, and the old world composes that:

Racism lays on two fundamental presumptions: that a relationship exists between physical attributes and excellent characteristics; that humankind is distinguishable into current and second rate stocks. Racism, in this way characterized, is a cutting edge origination, for, before the XVIth century, there was nothing in the life and thought of the West that can be portrayed as a bigot. To forestall misconception, a reasonable differentiation must be made among racism and ethnocentrism ... The Ancient Hebrews, in alluding to all who were not Hebrews as Gentiles, were enjoying ethnocentrism, not in racism. ... So it was with the Hellenes who designated all non-Hellenes— regardless of whether the wild Scythians or the Egyptians whom they recognized as their tutors in expressions of the human experience of development—Barbarians, the term signifying what was unusual or outside.

Bernard Lewis has likewise referred to history specialists and geographers of the Middle East and North Africa locale, including Al-Muqaddasi, Al-Jahiz, Al-Masudi, Abu Rayhan Biruni, Nasir al-Din al-Tusi, and Ibn Qutaybah. Although the Qur'an communicates no racial partiality, Lewis contends that ethnocentric bias later created among Arabs, for an assortment of reasons: their broad triumphs and slave exchange; the impact of Aristotelian thoughts concerning subjugation, which some Muslim logicians coordinated towards Zanj (Bantu) and Turkic people groups; and the effect of Judeo-Christian ideas in regards to divisions among humankind. The Afro-Arab writer Al-Jahiz, himself having a Zanj granddad, composed a book entitled Superiority of the Blacks to the Whites, and clarified why the Zanj were dark as far as natural determinism in the "On the Zanj" section of The Essays. By the fourteenth century, a critical number of slaves originated from sub-Saharan Africa; Lewis contends that this prompted any semblance of Egyptian student of history Al-Abshibi (1388–1446) composing that "[i]t is said that when the [black] slave is satisfied, he has sex when he is ravenous, he takes." According to Lewis, the fourteenth-century Tunisian researcher Ibn Khaldun likewise composed:

...past toward the South there is no human advancement in the best possible sense. There are just people who are nearer to moronic creatures than to sound creatures. They live in bushes and surrenders and eat herbs and ill-equipped grain. They as often as possible eat one another. They can't be viewed as individuals. In this manner, the Negro countries are, when in doubt, accommodating to bondage, because (Negroes) have little that is (basically) human and have characteristics that are very like those of imbecilic creatures, as we have expressed.

As it may, as indicated by Wesleyan University educator Abdelmajid Hannum, such mentalities were not pervasive until the eighteenth and nineteenth hundreds of years. He contends that a few records of Arabic writings, for example, those of Ibn Khaldun, were mistranslations by French Orientalists anticipating bigot and colonialist perspectives on the nineteenth century into their interpretations of medieval Arabic works. James E. Lindsay likewise contends that the idea of an Arab character itself didn't exist until present-day times.

Limpieza de Sangre

With the Umayyad Caliphate's victory of Hispania, attacking Muslim Berbers toppled the past Visigothic rulers. It made Al-Andalus, which added to the Golden time of Jewish culture, and went on for six centuries. It was trailed continuously long Reconquista, ended under the Catholic rulers Ferdinand V and Isabella I., The heritage Catholic Spaniards at that point, figured the Cleanliness of blood precept. During this time that the Western idea of highborn "nobility" developed in a racialized, strict and primitive setting, to stem the upward social versatility of the changed over New Christians. Robert Lacey clarifies:

It was the Spaniards who gave the idea that a blue's blood isn't red however blue. The Spanish respectability began coming to fruition around the ninth century in great military-style, involving land as warriors riding a horse. They were to proceed with the procedure for more than 500 years, tearing back segments of the landmass from its Moorish occupiers. An aristocrat showed his family by holding up his blade arm to show the filigree of pedigreed veins underneath his fair skin—verification that the darker looking foe had not sullied his introduction to the world. Sangre Azul, nobility, was along these lines a code word for being a white man—Spain's specific update that the refined strides of the privileged through history convey the somewhat less refined spoor of racism.

Following the removal of the Arabic Moors and the more significant part of the Sephardic Jews from the Iberian peninsula, the rest of the Jews and Muslims had to change over to Roman Catholicism, turning out to be "New Christians", who were here and there oppressed by the "Old Christians" in specific urban communities (counting Toledo), despite judgments by the Church and the State, which both invited the new rush. The Inquisition was done by individuals from the Dominican Order to get rid of the believers who despite everything rehearsed Judaism and Islam stealthily. The framework and belief system of the Limpieza de Sangre shunned bogus Christian proselytes from society to secure it against conspiracy. The leftovers of such enactment continued into the nineteenth century in military settings.

In Portugal, the legitimate differentiation among New and Old Christian was just finished through an official announcement gave by the Marquis of Pombal in 1772, right around three centuries after the usage of the bigot separation. The Limpieza de Sangre enactment was ordinary additionally during the colonization of the Americas, where it prompted the racial and primitive partition of people groups and social layers in the provinces. It was anyway regularly overlooked by and by, as the new areas required gifted individuals.

A sixteenth-century delineation by Flemish Protestant Theodor de Bry for Las Casas' Brevisima relación de la destrucción de las Indias, portraying Spanish barbarities during the success of Cuba.

Toward the finish of the Renaissance, the Valladolid banter (1550–1551), concerning the treatment of the locals of the "New World" pitted the Dominican monk and Bishop of Chiapas, Bartolomé de Las Casas, to another Dominican and Humanist thinker, Juan Ginés de Sepúlveda. The last contended that the Indians rehearsed personal penance of blameless people, savagery, and other such "wrongdoings against nature"; they were unsuitable and ought to be stifled using any means conceivable including war, accordingly diminishing them to servitude or serfdom was as per Catholic philosophy and natural law. Despite what might be expected, Bartolomé de Las Casas contended that the Amerindians were free men in the common request and merited a similar treatment as others, as per Catholic philosophy. It was one of the numerous contentions concerning racism, bondage, religion, and decent European quality that would emerge in the next hundreds of years and which brought about the enactment securing the locals. The wedding of Luisa de Abrego, a free dark residential hireling and Miguel, a white Segovian conquistador in 1565 in St. Augustine, is the primary known and recorded Christian marriage anyplace in the mainland United States.

Even though discrimination against Jews has a long history, identified with Christianity and local Egyptian or Greek religions (hostile to Judaism), racism itself is at times portrayed as a cutting edge wonder. In perspective on the French savant and history specialist Michel Foucault, the first plan of racism developed in the Early Modern time frame as the "talk of race battle", and a correct and political talk, which Foucault restricted to the philosophical and juridical conversation of sway. Then again, for example, Chinese self-ID as a "yellow race" originated before such European racial ideas.

This European examination, which initially showed up in Great Britain, was then carried on in France by such individuals as Boulainvilliers, Nicolas Fréret, and afterwards, during the 1789 French Revolution, Sieyès, and a short time later, Augustin Thierry and Cournot. Boulainvilliers, who made the framework of such supremacist talk in medieval France, considered the "race" as being something nearer to the feeling of a "country", that is, in his time, the "race" implied the "individuals".

He thought about France as being separated between different countries – the bound together country state is a time misplacement here – which themselves shaped diverse "races". Boulainvilliers contradicted the outright government, which attempted to sidestep the nobility by setting up an immediate relationship to the Third Estate. In this manner, he built up the hypothesis that the French nobles were the relatives of outside intruders, whom he called the "Franks". At the same time, as per him, the Third Estate established the autochthonous, vanquished Gallo-Romans, who were ruled by the Frankish nobility as an outcome of the privilege of victory. New present-day racism was against patriotism and the country express: the Comte de Montlosier, in a state of banishment during the French Revolution, who acquired Boulainvilliers' talk on the "Nordic race" just like the French nobility that attacked the plebeian "Gauls", along these lines demonstrated his scorn for the Third Estate, calling it "this new individual conceived of slaves ... blend everything being equal and all things considered".

Nineteenth-century

While nineteenth-century racism turned out to be firmly entwined with patriotism, prompting the ethnic patriot talk that distinguished the "race" with the "society", inspiring such developments as skillet Germanism, dish Turkism, container Arabism, and dish Slavism, medieval racism unequivocally separated the country into different non-organic "races", which were believed to be the result of authentic victories and social clashes. Michel Foucault followed the parentage of present-day racism to this medieval "verifiable and political talk of race battle". As indicated by him, it isolated itself in the nineteenth century as per two adversary lines: on the one hand, it was fused by racists, scientists and eugenicists, who gave it the cutting edge feeling of "race", and they additionally changed this popular talk into a "state racism" (e.g., Nazism). Then again, Marxism additionally held onto this talk established on suspicion of a political battle that gave the genuine motor of history and kept on acting underneath the apparent harmony. Along these lines, Marxists changed the essentialist idea of "race" into the recorded thought of "class battle", characterized by socially organized positions: entrepreneur or common. In The Will to Knowledge (1976), Foucault broke down another adversary of the "race battle" talk: Sigmund Freud's analysis, which contradicted the idea of "blood heredity", common in the nineteenth-century supremacist talk.

Writers, for example, Hannah Arendt, in her 1951 book The Origins of Totalitarianism, have said that the bigot philosophy (mainstream racism) which created toward the finish of the nineteenth century legitimized the colonialist triumphs of outside regions and the abominations that occasionally went with them. Rudyard Kipling's sonnet, The White Man's Burden (1899), is one of the more acclaimed representations of the faith in the inborn predominance of the European culture over the remainder of the world. However, it is additionally thought to be a humorous evaluation of such colonialism. Bigot philosophy, in this manner, legitimized the victory and joining of remote domains into a realm, which was viewed as a compassionate commitment mostly because of these supremacist convictions.

A late-nineteenth-century delineation from Ireland from One or Two Neglected Points of View by H. Strickland Constable shows supposed comparability between "Irish Iberian", and "Negro" includes rather than the "higher" "Old English Teutonic".

Be that as it may, during the nineteenth century, Western European provincial forces were associated with the concealment of the Arab slave exchange Africa, just as in the cover-up of the slave exchange West Africa. A few Europeans during the timeframe protested shameful acts that happened in individual states and campaigned in the interest of native people groups. Consequently, when the Hottentot Venus was shown in England at the start of the nineteenth century, the African Association openly restricted itself to the presentation. That year that Kipling distributed his sonnet, Joseph Conrad distributed Heart of Darkness (1899), and away from of the Congo Free State, which was claimed by Leopold II of Belgium.

Instances of racial speculations utilized to incorporate the production of the Hamitic Ethno-phonetic gathering during the European investigation of Africa. It was then limited by Karl

Friedrich Lepsius (1810–1877) to non-Semitic Afro-Asiatic dialects.

The term Hamite was applied to various populaces inside North Africa, principally containing Ethiopians, Eritreans, Somalis, Berbers, and the antiquated Egyptians. Hamites were viewed as Caucasoid people groups who presumably began in either Arabia or Asia based on their social, physical and etymological similitudes with the people groups of those territories. Europeans considered Hamites to be more socialized than Sub-Saharan Africans, and increasingly similar to themselves and Semitic people groups. In the initial 66% of the twentieth century, the Hamitic race was, indeed, viewed as one of the parts of the Caucasian race, alongside the Indo-Europeans, Semites, and the Mediterranean.

Be that as it may, the Hamitic people groups themselves were regularly esteemed to have bombed as rulers, which was generally attributed to interbreeding with Negroes. In the mid-twentieth century, the German researcher Carl Meinhof (1857–1944) asserted that the Bantu race was framed by a merger of Hamitic and Negro races. The Hottentots (Nama or Khoi) were shaped by the alliance of Hamitic and Bushmen (San) races—both being named these days as Khoisan people groups.

One out of a progression of banners assaulting Radical Republicans on the issue of the dark testimonial gave during the Pennsylvania gubernatorial appointment of 1866.

In the US in the nineteenth century, the American Colonization Society was built up as the essential vehicle for recommendations to return dark Americans to more prominent opportunity and equity in Africa. The colonization exertion came about because of a blend of thought processes with its organizer Henry Clay expressing that "unconquerable partiality coming about because of their shading, they never could amalgamate with the free whites of this nation. It was alluring, accordingly, as it regarded them, and the buildup of the number of inhabitants in the nation, to deplete them off". Racism spread all through the New World in the late nineteenth century and mid-twentieth century. White capping, which began in Indiana in the late nineteenth century, before long spread all through all of North America, making numerous African workers escape from the land they chipped away at. In the US, during the 1860s, bigot banners were utilized during political races. In one of these bigot banners, a dark man is delineated relaxing inactively in the closer view as one white man furrows his field and another cleaves wood. Going with marks are: "In the perspiration of thy face shalt thou eat thy bread", and "The white people work to keep his youngsters and make good on his duties." The dark man ponders, "Whar is de use for me to fill in as long as dey make dese allocations." Above in a cloud is a picture of the "Freedman's Bureau! Negro Estimate of Freedom!" The authority is imagined as an enormous domed structure taking after the U.S. Legislative hall and is engraved "Opportunity and No Work". Its segments and dividers are marked, "Sweets", "Rum, Gin, Whiskey", "Sugar

Plums", "Sluggishness", "White Women", "Lack of concern", "White Sugar", "Inaction, etc. On June 5, 1873, Sir Francis Galton, recognized English adventurer and cousin of Charles Darwin, wrote in a letter to The Times:

I propose to make the support of Chinese settlements of Africa a piece of our national approach, in the conviction that the Chinese migrants would keep up their position, yet that they would increase and their relatives override the second rate Negro race. I ought to anticipate that the African seaboard, presently scantily involved by lazy, palavering savages, may in a couple of years be rented by innovative, request adoring Chinese, living either as a semidetached reliance of China, or, in all likelihood in ideal opportunity under their law.

Twentieth-century

The Nazi party, which held onto power in the 1933 German decisions and kept up a tyranny over quite a bit of Europe until the End of World War II on the European landmass, regarded the Germans to be a piece of an Aryan "ace race" (Herrenvolk), who in this manner reserved the privilege to grow their domain and oppressor murder individuals from different races considered sub-par.

The racial belief system brought about by the Nazis evaluated people on size of unadulterated Aryan to non-Aryan, with the last saw as subhuman. At the highest point of the size of unadulterated Aryans were Germans and other Germanic people groups including the Dutch, Scandinavians, and the English just as different people groups, for example, some Italians and the French, who were supposed to have an appropriate admixture of Germanic blood. Nazi arrangements named Romani individuals, minorities, and Slavs (chiefly Poles, Serbs, Russians, Belarusians, Ukrainians and Czechs) as second rate non-Aryan subhumans. Jews were at the base of the chain of importance, considered barbaric and along these lines disgraceful of life.

The Nazis believed most Slavs to be non-Aryan Untermenschen. The Menace of the Under-man. Slavic countries, for example, the Slovaks, Bulgarians, and Croats, who worked together with Nazi Germany were seen as ethnically better than different Slavs, for the most part, because of pseudoscientific hypotheses about these countries having an impressive admixture of Germanic blood. In the mystery plan Generalplan Ost ("Master Plan East") the Nazis set out to oust, subjugate, or annihilate most Slavic individuals to give "living space" for Germans, anyway Nazi arrangement towards Slavs changed during World War II because of labour deficiencies which required restricted Slavic cooperation in the Waffen-SS. Noteworthy atrocities were carried out against Slavs, especially Poles, and Soviet POWs had a far higher death rate than their American and British partners because of purposeful disregard and abuse. Between June 1941 to March 1942, the Nazis murdered an expected 2.8 million Red Army POWs, whom they saw as "subhuman".

During the strengthening of binds with Nazi Germany during the 1930s, Ante Pavelić and the Ustaše and their concept of the Croatian country turned out to be progressively race-arranged. The Ustaše perspective on the national and racial character, just as the hypothesis of Serbs as a substandard race, was affected by Croatian patriots and learned people from the finish of the nineteenth and the start of the twentieth century. Serbs were the essential objective of racial laws and murders in the manikin express, the NDH, Jews and Roma were likewise focused on. The Ustaše acquainted the rules with strip Serbs of their citizenship, occupations, and assets. During the slaughter in the NDH, Serbs endured among the most elevated loss rates in Europe during World War II, while the NDH was one of the most deadly systems in the twentieth century.

German commendation for America's institutional racism was constant all through the mid-1930s, and Nazi legal counsellors were supporters of the utilization of American models. Race-based U.S. citizenship laws and hostile to miscegenation laws (no race blending) legitimately roused the Nazi's two head Nuremberg racial laws – the Citizenship Law and the Blood Law. Hitler's 1925 diary Mein Kampf was brimming with profound respect for America's treatment of "coloureds". Nazi development eastbound was gone with the conjuring of America's pioneer extension westbound, with the going with activities toward the Native Americans. In 1928, Hitler commended Americans for having "gunned down a large number of Redskins to two or three hundred thousand, and now holds the humble remainder under perception in an enclosure." On Nazi Germany's development eastbound, in 1941, Hitler expressed, "Our Mississippi must be the Volga." A sign posted over a bar that peruses "No brew offered to Indians". Birney, Montana, 1941.

Racial oppression was prevailing in the U.S. up to social liberties development. On the U.S. migration laws preceding 1965, humanist Stephen Klineberg referred to the law as obviously proclaiming "that Northern Europeans are an unrivalled subspecies of the white race." While hostile to Asian racism was implanted in U.S. governmental issues and culture in the mid-twentieth century, Indians were likewise racialized for their anticolonialism, with U.S. authorities, giving them a role as a "Hindu" hazard, pushing for Western royal development abroad. The Naturalization Act of 1790 restricted U.S. citizenship to whites just, and in the 1923 case, the US v. Bhagat Singh Thind, the Supreme Court decided that high station Hindus were not "white people" and were hence racially ineligible for naturalized citizenship. It was after the Act of 1946 that a quantity of 100 Indians for every year could move to the U.S. what's more, become residents. The Nationality and immigration Act of 1965 significantly opened section to the U.S. to outsiders other than regular Northern European and Germanic gatherings. Subsequently, it would radically adjust the segment blend in the U.S.

Genuine race revolts in Durban among Indians and Zulus emitted in 1949. Ne Win's ascent to control in Burma in 1962 and his determined mistreatment of "inhabitant outsiders" prompted a mass migration of somewhere in the range of 300,000 Burmese Indians. They moved to get away from racial segregation and discount nationalization of private endeavors a couple of years after the fact, in 1964. The Zanzibar Revolution of January 12, 1964, shut down the nearby Arab tradition. A great many Arabs and Indians in Zanzibar were slaughtered in uproars, and thousands more were confined or fled the island. In August 1972, Ugandan President Idi Amin began the seizure of properties possessed by Asians and Europeans. Around the same time, Amin ethnically washed down Uganda's Asians, allowing them 90 days to leave the nation. Soon after World War II, the South African National Party assumed responsibility for the legislature in South Africa. Somewhere between 1948 and 1994, the politically-sanctioned racial segregation system occurred. This system put together its philosophy concerning the racial partition of whites and non-whites, including the inconsistent privileges of non-whites. A few fights and brutality happened during the battle against politically-sanctioned racial segregation, and the most celebrated of these incorporate the Sharpeville Massacre in 1960, the Soweto uprising in 1976, the Church Street besieging of 1983, and the Cape Town harmony walk of 1989.

Contemporary

During the Congo Civil War (1998–2003), Pygmy individuals were pursued down like game creatures and eaten. The two sides in the war viewed them as "subhuman" and some state their substance can give enchanted forces. UN human rights activists announced in 2003 that renegades had completed demonstrations of savagery. Safari Makelo, an agent of the Mbuti dwarfs, has asked the UN Security Council to perceive savagery as both an unspeakable atrocity and a demonstration of decimation. A report discharged by the United Nations Committee on the Elimination of Racial Discrimination denounces Botswana's treatment of the 'Bushmen' as supremacist. In 2008, the court of the 15-country Southern African Development Community (SADC) blamed Zimbabwean President Robert Mugabe for having a supremacist disposition towards white individuals.

The mass exhibits and uproars against African understudies in Nanjing, China, endured from December 1988 to January 1989. Bar proprietors in focal Beijing had been constrained by the police "not to serve dark individuals or Mongolians" during the 2008 Olympics, as the cops connected these ethnic gatherings with illegal prostitution and medication dealing. In November 2009, British paper The Guardian revealed that Lou Jing, of blended Chinese and African parentage, had developed as the most celebrated ability show challenger in China and has become the subject of extreme discussion as a result of her skin shading.

Her consideration in the media opened good talks about racism in China and racial preference.

Somewhere in the range of 70,000 dark African Mauritanians were ousted from Mauritania in the late 1980s. In Sudan, dark African hostages in the conventional war were regularly oppressed, and female detainees were frequently explicitly manhandled. Some have portrayed the Darfur struggle as a racial issue. In October 2006, Niger reported that it would surrender the around 150,000 Arabs living in the Diffa locale of eastern Niger to Chad. While the legislature gathered Arabs in anticipation of the extradition, two young ladies kicked the bucket, purportedly in the wake of escaping Government powers, and three ladies endured unnatural birth cycles. The wore out stays of Govinda's Indian Restaurant in Fiji, May 2000.

The Jakarta uproars of May 1998 focused on numerous Chinese Indonesians. The counter Chinese enactment was in the Indonesian constitution until 1998. Disdain against Chinese specialists has prompted vicious encounters in Africa and Oceania. Hostile to Chinese revolting, including a considerable number of individuals, broke out in Papua New Guinea in May 2009. Indo-Fijians endured rough assaults after the Fiji overthrow in 2000. Non-indigenous residents of Fiji are dependent upon segregation. Racial divisions additionally exist in Guyana, Malaysia, Trinidad and Tobago, Madagascar, and South Africa.

Diminish Bouckaert, the Human Rights Watch's crises executive said in a meeting that "supremacist disdain" is the main inspiration driving the savagery against Rohingya Muslims in Myanmar.

With the point of saving the segment cosmetics of the Zionist state, components inside Israeli society have been blamed for unfair conduct against the Arab populace and toward different Jews of a darker appearance. These people group excessively possess worker positions with the workforce. Allegations of racism have likewise included anti-conception medication arrangements, instruction, and lodging separation.

One type of racism in the United States was implemented racial isolation, which existed until the 1960s when it was prohibited in the Civil Rights Act of 1964. It has been contended that this division of races keeps on existing accepted today in various structures, for example, absence of access to credits and assets or segregation by police and other government authorities.

The 2016 Pew Research survey found that Italians, specifically, hold robust enemy of Roma sees, with 82% of Italians communicating negative sentiments about Roma. In Greece, there are 67%, in Hungary, 64%, in France, 61%, in Spain, 49%, in Poland, 47%, in the UK, 45%, in Sweden, 42%, in Germany, 40%, and in the Netherlands, 37%, that have a negative perspective on Roma. A study led by Harvard University found the Czech Republic, Lithuania, Belarus and Ukraine have the most grounded racial inclination towards dark individuals in Europe. In contrast, Serbia and Slovenia have a most vulnerable racial predisposition, trailed by Bosnia and Herzegovina, Croatia and Ireland.

Logical racism

The advanced organic meaning of race created in the nineteenth century with logical supremacist speculations. The term consistent racism alludes to the utilization of science to legitimize and bolster bigot convictions, which returns to the mid-eighteenth century. However, it increased a significant portion of its impact in the mid-nineteenth century, during the New Imperialism time frame. Otherwise called academic racism, such speculations previously expected to conquer the Church's protection from positivist records of history and its help of monogenism, the idea that every individual was started from similar progenitors, as per creationist records of history.

These bigot speculations set forth on logical theory were joined with unilineal hypotheses of social advancement, which hypothesized the predominance of the European human progress over the remainder of the world. Moreover, they much of the time utilized the possibility of "natural selection", a term begat by Herbert Spencer in 1864, related with thoughts of rivalry, which were named social Darwinism during the 1940s. Charles Darwin himself contradicted the possibility of unbending racial contrasts in The Descent of Man (1871), in which he contended that people were every one of one animal varieties, sharing normal plummet. He perceived racial contrasts as assortments of humankind. He underscored the nearby similitudes between individuals of all races in intellectual capacities, tastes, manners and propensities, while as yet differentiating the way of life of the "most minimal savages" with European human progress.

Toward the finish of the nineteenth century, advocates of logical racism entwined themselves with genetic counselling talks of "degeneration of the race" and "blood heredity". Henceforth, consistent supremacist talks could be characterized as a mix of polygenism, unilateralism, social Darwinism, and eugenism. They discovered their logical authenticity on human physical sciences, anthropometry, craniometry, phrenology, physiognomy, and others currently ruined teaches to plan supremacist preferences.

Before being excluded in the twentieth century by the American school of social humanities (Franz Boas, and so forth.), the British school of social humanities (Bronisław Malinowski, Alfred Radcliffe-Brown, and so forth.), the French school of ethnology (Claude Lévi-Strauss, and so on.), just as the disclosure of the neo-Darwinian union, such sciences, specifical anthropometry, were utilized to conclude practices and mental attributes from outward, physical appearances.

The neo-Darwinian amalgamation, first created during the 1930s, in the long run, prompted a quality-focused perspective on development during the 1960s. As indicated by the Human Genome Project, a complete mapping of human DNA to date shows that there is no unmistakable hereditary premise to racial gatherings. While a few qualities are increasingly standard in specific populaces, there are no qualities that exist in all individuals from one populace and no individuals from some other.

Heredity and genetic counselling

The principal hypothesis of selective breeding was created in 1869 by Francis Galton (1822–1911), who utilized the then-well known idea of degeneration. He applied insights to contemplate social contrasts and the affirmed "legacy of knowledge", foretelling future employments of "knowledge testing" by the anthropometry school. Such speculations were distinctively depicted by the essayist Émile Zola (1840–1902), who began distributing in 1871, a twenty-novel cycle, Les Rougon-Macquart, where he connected heredity to conduct. In this way, Zola depicted the high-conceived Rougons as those engaged with governmental issues (Son Excellence Eugène Rougon) and medication (Le Docteur Pascal) and the low-conceived Macquarts as those lethally falling into liquor abuse (L'Assommoir), prostitution (Nana), and manslaughter (La Bête Humaine).

During the ascent of Nazism in Germany, a few researchers in Western countries attempted to expose the system's racial speculations. A couple contended against bigot belief systems and segregation, regardless of whether they put stock in the supposed presence of natural races. Be that as it may, in the fields of humanities and science, these were minority positions until the mid-twentieth century. As indicated by the 1950 UNESCO articulation, The Race Question, a universal task to expose bigot hypotheses had endeavored in the mid-1930s. In any case, this undertaking had been deserted. In this way, in 1950, UNESCO pronounced that it had continued:

up once more, following a slip by of fifteen years, a task that the International Committee on Intellectual Cooperation has wished to help through however that it needed to forsake in reverence to the settlement arrangement of the pre-war period. The race question had gotten one of the turns of the Nazi belief system and approach. Masaryk and Beneš stepped up of requiring a meeting to restore in the brains and hearts of men wherever reality with regards to race Nazi purposeful publicity had the option to proceed with its injurious work unopposed by the authority of a worldwide association.

The Third Reich's racial arrangements, its genetic counselling programs and the elimination of Jews in the Holocaust, just as the Romani individuals in the Porrajmos (the Romani Holocaust) and others minorities prompted an adjustment in suppositions about a logical investigation into the race after the war. Changes inside logical controls, for example, the ascent of the Boasian school of human sciences in the United States added to this move. These hypotheses were emphatically reproved in the 1950 UNESCO proclamation, marked by universally famous researchers, and titled The Race Question.

Polygenism and racial typologies

Works, for example, Arthur de Gobineau's An Essay on the Inequality of the Human Races (1853–1855) might be considered as one of the main hypotheses of this new racism, established on an essentialist thought of race, which contradicted the previous racial talk, of Boulainvilliers for instance, which found in sports. A general sense recorded reality, which changed after some time. Gobineau, along these lines, endeavored to outline racism inside the details of natural contrasts among people, giving it the authenticity of science.

Gobineau's speculations would be extended in France by Georges Vacher de Lapouge (1854–1936's) typology of races, who distributed in 1899 The Aryan and his Social Role, where he asserted that the white "Aryan race" "dolichocephalic", was against the "brachycephalic" race, of whom the "Jew" was the model. Vacher de Lapouge in this manner made a progressive order of tracks, wherein he recognized the "Homo europaeus (Teutonic, Protestant, and so forth.), the "Homo alpinus" (Auvergnat, Turkish, and so forth.), lastly the "Homo mediterraneus" (Neapolitan, Andalus, and so on.) He absorbed races and social classes, taking into account that the French privileged was a portrayal of the Homo europaeus, while the lower quality spoke to the Homo alpinus. Applying Galton's genetic counselling to his hypothesis of races, Vacher de Lapouge's "selections" pointed first at accomplishing the demolition of exchange unionists, viewed as a "degenerate"; second, making sorts of man each bound to one end, to forestall any contestation of work conditions. His "anthroposociology" subsequently planned for blocking social clash by building up a fixed, various leveled social request.

That year, William Z. Ripley utilized the same racial grouping in The Races of Europe (1899), which would have an extraordinary impact in the United States. Other logical creators incorporate H.S. Chamberlain toward the finish of the nineteenth century (a British resident who naturalized himself as German in light of his deference for the "Aryan race") and Madison Grant, a eugenicist and creator of The Passing of the Great Race (1916). Madison Grant gave measurements to the Immigration Act of 1924, which severely limited movement of Jews, Slavs, and southern Europeans, who were therefore blocked in looking to get away from Nazi Germany.

Human zoos or individual shows

Human zoos (called "Individuals Shows"), were significant methods for reinforcing famous racism by interfacing it to logical racism: they were the two objects of open interest and human sciences and anthropometry. Joice Heth, an African American slave, was shown by P.T. Barnum in 1836, a couple of years after the display of Saartjie Baartman, the "Hottentot Venus", in England. Such shows got basic in the New Imperialism time frame and remained so until World War II. Carl Hagenbeck, the innovator of the advanced zoos, displayed creatures alongside people who were considered "savages".

Congolese dwarf Ota Benga was shown in 1906 by eugenicist Madison Grant, leader of the Bronx Zoo, as an endeavor to outline the "missing connection" among people and orangutans. In this way, racism was attached to Darwinism, making a social Darwinist belief system that attempted to ground itself in Darwin's logical revelations. The 1931 Paris Colonial Exhibition showed Kanaks from New Caledonia. A "Congolese town" was in plain view as late as 1958 at the Brussels' World Fair.

Hypotheses about the birthplaces of racism

Transformative therapists John Tooby and Leda Cosmides were confused by the way that in the US, the race is one of the three attributes regularly utilized in a word portrayals of people (the others are age and sex). They contemplated that common choice would not have supported the advancement of a sense for utilizing race as a grouping, because for the vast majority of humankind's history, people never experienced individuals from different races. Tooby and Cosmides estimated that cutting edge; individuals use the track as an intermediary (crude but effective marker) for alliance participation since a superior than-arbitrary theory about "which side" someone else is on will be useful if one doesn't know ahead of time.

Their associate Robert Kurzban structured an investigation whose outcomes seemed to help this theory. Utilizing the Memory disarray convention, they gave subjects pictures of people and sentences, supposedly spoken by these people, which introduced different sides of a discussion. The mistakes that the items made in reviewing who said what showed that they in some cases miscredited an announcement to a speaker of a similar race, although they additionally at times mis-ascribed, a letter to a speaker "on a similar side" as the "right" speaker. In a second run of the test, the group additionally recognized the "sides" in the discussion by apparel of comparative hues; and for this situation the impact of racial closeness in causing botches nearly disappeared, being supplanted by the shade of their attire. The first gathering of subjects, without any intimations from garments, utilized race as a visual manual for think about who was on which side of the discussion; the second gathering of subjects used the garments shading as their principle visible sign, and the impact of the race turned out to be little.

Some examination recommends that ethnocentric reasoning may have added to the improvement of participation. Political specialists Ross Hammond and Robert Axelrod made a PC recreation wherein virtual people were haphazardly allocated one of an assortment of skin hues, and afterwards one of a variety of exchanging systems: be partially blind, favour those of your shading, or favour those of different tones. They found that the ethnocentric people bunched together, at that point developed until all the non-ethnocentric people were cleared out.

In The Selfish Gene, developmental researcher Richard Dawkins composes that "Blood-fights and between-group fighting are effectively interpretable as far as Hamilton's hereditary hypothesis." Dawkins composes that racial partiality, while not developmentally versatile, "could be deciphered as silly speculation of a family chosen propensity to relate to people truly taking after oneself, and to be awful to people diverse in appearance." Simulation-based tests in transformative game hypothesis have endeavored to clarify the choice of ethnocentric-technique phenotypes.

Despite help for transformative hypotheses identifying with an inborn root of racism, different examinations have recommended racism is related to lower insight and less various companion bunches during youth. A neuroimaging concentrate on amygdala action during racial coordinating exercises saw expanded action as relevant to young age just as less racially different companion gatherings, which the creator close propose an educated part of racism. A meta investigation of neuroimaging contemplates discovered amygdala movement connected to expanded scores on correct proportions of racial inclination. It was additionally contended amygdala movement in light of racial boosts speaks to expanded danger discernment as opposed to the conventional hypothesis of the amygdala action spoke to ingroup-outgroup preparing. Racism has additionally been related to lower youth IQ in an examination of 15,000 individuals in the UK.

State-supported racism

State racism – that is, the organizations and practices of a country express that are grounded in bigot philosophy – has assumed a significant job in all examples of pilgrim imperialism, from the United States to Australia. It additionally thought a remarkable position in the Nazi German system, in fundamentalist systems all through Europe, and during the early long periods of Japan's Shōwa period. These administrations upheld and executed belief systems and strategies that were supremacist, xenophobic, and, on account of Nazism, destructive.

The Nuremberg Race Laws of 1935 precluded sexual relations between any Aryan and Jew, considering it Rassenschande, "racial contamination". The Nuremberg Laws stripped all Jews, even quarter-and half-Jews (second and first degree Mischlings), of their German citizenship. This implied they had no fundamental residents' privileges, e.g., the option to cast a ballot. In 1936, Jews were prohibited from every single proficient employment, adequately keeping them from having any impact in training, governmental issues, advanced education, and industry. On 15 November 1938, Jewish kids were restricted from going to typical schools. By April 1939, about every single Jewish organization had either crumpled under budgetary tension and declining benefits, or had been convinced to sell out to the Nazi government. This further decreased their privileges as people; they were from various perspectives authoritatively isolated from the German masses. Comparable laws existed in Bulgaria – The Law for assurance of the country, Hungary, Romania, and Austria.

Administrative state racism is known to host been authorized by the National Get-together of South Africa during its Apartheid system somewhere in the range of 1948 and 1994. Here, a progression of Apartheid enactment was gone through the legal frameworks to make it lawful for white South Africans to have rights which were better than those of non-white South Africans. Non-white South Africans were not permitted contribution in any administering issues, including casting a ballot; access to quality social insurance; the arrangement of essential administrations, including clean water; power; just as access to sufficient tutoring. Non-white South Africans were additionally kept from getting to certain open regions, from utilizing sure accessible transportation, and were required to live just in certain assigned zones. Non-white South Africans were burdened uniquely in contrast to white South Africans, and they were likewise required to carry on them consistently extra documentation, which later got known as "dom goes", to ensure their non-white South African citizenship. These administrative racial laws were annulled through a progression of equivalent human rights laws which were passed toward the finish of the Apartheid period in the mid-1990s.

Hostile to racism

Hostile to racism incorporates convictions, activities, developments, and strategies which are received or created to restrict racism. All in all, it advances a populist society wherein individuals are not victimized based on race. Developments, for example, the social equality development and the Anti-Apartheid Movement were instances of against supremacist developments. Peaceful obstruction is in some cases held onto as a component of hostile to supremacist developments, although this was not generally the situation. Detest wrongdoing laws, governmental policy regarding minorities in society, and bans on bigot discourse are likewise instances of government arrangement which is proposed to smother racism.

Racism in the United States

Racism in the United States had existed since the provincial time when white Americans were given lawfully or socially authorized benefits and rights. At the same time, these equivalent rights were denied to different races and minorities. European Americans—especially well-off white Anglo-Saxon Protestants—delighted in elite benefits in issues of instruction, movement, casting ballot rights, citizenship, land procurement, and criminal technique all through American history. Non-Protestant migrants from Europe, uniquely the Irish, Poles, and Italians, regularly endured xenophobic prohibition and different types of ethnicity-based segregation in American culture until the late nineteenth and mid-twentieth hundreds of years. Also, bunches, like Jews and Arabs, have confronted ceaseless discrimination in the United States. Therefore, a few people who have a place with these gatherings are not recognized as white. African Americans faced limitations on their political, social, and monetary opportunity all through quite a bit of US history. Local Americans have encountered destruction, constrained expulsions, slaughters, and separation. Truly, Hispanics have likewise experienced consistent racism in the US. Moreover, South, Southeast, and East Asians have additionally been victimized. Pacific Islander Americans also suffer separation and minimization.

Major racially and ethnically organized establishments and appearances of racism have included destruction, bondage, isolation, Native American reservations, Native American all-inclusive schools, migration and naturalization laws, and internment camps. Formal racial separation was generally restricted by the mid-twentieth century, and after some time, it came to be seen as being socially and ethically unsatisfactory. Racial governmental issues stay a significant marvel, and racism keeps on being reflected in financial imbalance. Racial delineation keeps on happening in work, lodging, instruction, loaning, and government.

In perspective on the United Nations and the U.S. Human Rights Network, "segregation in the United States pervades all parts of life and stretches out to all networks of shading." While the idea of the perspectives which are held by ordinary Americans has changed altogether in recent decades, overviews which have been led by associations, for example, ABC News have discovered that even in current America, countless Americans concede that they hold oppressive perspectives. For instance, a 2007 article by ABC expressed that around one out of ten Americans acknowledged that they hold preferences against Hispanic and Latino Americans and around one out of four Americans conceded that they hold partialities against Arab Americans. A 2018 YouGov/Economist survey found that 17% of Americans restrict interracial marriage, with 19% of individuals from "other" ethnic gatherings, 18% of blacks, 17% of whites, and 15% of Hispanics contradicting it.

A few Americans saw the presidential bid of Barack Obama, who filled in as leader of the United States from 2009 to december 2017 and was the country's first dark president, as a sign that the state had entered another, post-racial period. In November 2009, the conservative populist radio and TV have Lou Dobbs asserted, "We are currently in a 21st-century post-divided, post-racial society." after two months, Chris Matthews, an MSNBC have, said that President Obama, "is post-racial by all appearances. You know, I overlooked he was dark today around evening time for 60 minutes." The appointment of President Donald Trump in 2016 has been seen by certain pundits as a supremacist reaction against the election of Barack Obama, with CNN analyst Van Jones considering his political decision a "whitelash".

During the 2010s, American culture has kept on encountering elevated levels of racism and separation. One new wonder has been the ascent of the "extreme right" development: a white patriot alliance that looks for the removal of sexual and racial minorities from the United States. In August 2017, these gatherings went to a convention in Charlottesville, Virginia, expected to bring together different white patriot groups. During the meeting, a racial oppressor demonstrator drove his vehicle into a gathering of counter-dissenters, slaughtering one individual and harming 19.

Racism

Racism is an arranged type of mistreatment which is created by individuals from one race to aggrieve individuals from another race. Biased perspectives existed between races for a large number of years, yet arranged racial abuse initially emerged during the 1600s alongside free enterprise. Before this period, racism didn't exist, and in numerous societies, slaves were usually taken because of military triumph. In any case, when European brokers found that their boss innovation gave them an enormous bit of leeway in Africa, including their cruising boats and guns, they started to loot Africa's riches and take slaves. Slave masters and slave proprietors both attempted to legitimize the act of subjugation by persuading themselves that before their African slaves were caught and oppressed, they had no past culture and lived like savages, a false presumption. White European Americans who took an interest in the slave business attempted to legitimize their financial abuse of dark individuals by making a "logical" hypothesis of white prevalence and obscure mediocrity. One such slave proprietor was Thomas Jefferson, and it was his call for science to decide the self-evident "mediocrity" of blacks that is viewed as "a critical stage in the development of logical racism." This was the beginning of arranged racism in the United States.

African Americans Racism

The Atlantic slave exchange had a monetary establishment. The prevailing philosophy among the European world-class who organized national approach all through the age of the Atlantic slave exchange was mercantilism, the conviction that national strategy ought to be revolved around storing up military influence and financial riches. Settlements were wellsprings of mineral wealth and yields, to be utilized to the colonizing nation's favourable position. Using Europeans for work in the states demonstrated impractically costly, just as destructive to the household work flexibly of the colonizing countries. Instead, the settlements imported African slaves, who were "accessible in huge numbers at costs that made ranch farming in the Americas productive".

It is additionally contended that alongside the financial thought processes which underly subjection in the Americas, European world diagrams assumed a massive job in the subjugation of Africans. As per this view, the European in-bunch for altruistic conduct incorporated the sub-mainland, while African and American Indian societies had a progressively confined meaning of "an insider". While neither one of the schemas has inalienable prevalence, the favourable mechanical position of Europeans turned into an asset to disperse the conviction that underscored their compositions, that non-Europeans could be oppressed.

With the ability to spread their schematic portrayal of the world, Europeans could force an implicit understanding, ethically allowing three centuries of African bondage. While the deterioration of this tacit agreement by the eighteenth century prompted abolitionism, it is contended that the evacuation of boundaries to "insider status" is a reasonable procedure, uncompleted even today (2017).

Because of the above mentioned, the Atlantic slave exchange flourished. As per gauges in the Trans-Atlantic Slave Trade Database, somewhere in the range of 1626 and 1860 more than 470,000 slaves were coercively moved from Africa to what is currently the United States. Before the Civil War, eight serving presidents claimed slaves, a training which was ensured by the U.S. Constitution. Giving riches to the white world-class, roughly one out of four Southern families held slaves before the Civil War. As indicated by the 1860 U.S. statistics, there were around 385,000 slave proprietors out of a white populace of roughly 7 million in the slave states.

Gatherings of outfitted white men, called slave watches, observed oppressed African Americans. First settled in South Carolina in 1704, the slave watches' capacity was to police slaves, particularly wanderers. Slave proprietors dreaded slaves may sort out a revolt or defiance, so state volunteer armies were framed to give a military order structure and control inside the slave watches to distinguish, experience, and pound any composed slave gatherings that may prompt revolt or insubordination.

Steps toward the cancellation of bondage

During the 1820s and 1830s, the A.C.S. had as its crucial free dark Americans to where they could appreciate the unique opportunity in Africa, In 1821 the A.C.S. set up the settlement of Liberia, helping a great many previous African-American slaves and free dark individuals (with enacted limits) to move there from the United States. A few slaves were manumitted (liberated) on condition that they emigrate. The slave states made no mystery that they needed to dispose of free blacks, whom they accept compromised their venture, the slaves, empowering departures and rebellions. The help for the ACS was inherently Southern. The originator of the ACS, Henry Clay of Kentucky, expressed that on account of "unconquerable preference coming about because of their shading, they never could amalgamate with the free whites of this nation. It was attractive, consequently, as it regarded them, and the buildup of the number of inhabitants in the nation, to deplete them off".

Even though in 1820, the Atlantic slave exchange was likened with theft, deserving of death, the act of asset bondage kept on existing in the United States for an additional 35 years. The residential slave exchange – "trading" slaves south from Maryland and Virginia, which had surpluses; see Franklin and Armfield Office – was a significant financial action in the U.S.

which went on until the 1860s. Oppress relatives would be separated never to see or know about one another again. Somewhere in the range of 1830 and 1840, about 250,000 slaves were taken across state lines. During the 1850s more than 193,000 were shipped, and students of history gauge about one million altogether had to relocate.

The history specialist Ira Berlin considered this constrained movement of slaves the "Second Middle Passage" since it duplicated a large number of indistinguishable abhorrence from the Middle Passage. These deals of slaves separated numerous families, with Berlin composing that whether slaves were straightforwardly removed or lived in dread that they or their families would be automatically moved, "the huge expelling damaged dark individuals". People lost their association with families and tribes. Added to the previous settlers joining slaves from various clans, numerous ethnic Africans lost their insight into fluctuating ancestral inceptions in Africa. Most plummeted from families who had been in the U.S. for some ages.

The Emancipation Proclamation

Compelling January 1, 1863, President Lincoln expressed in his Emancipation Proclamation: "That on the primary day of January in the time of our Lord, one thousand 800 and sixty-three, all people held as slaves inside any State, or assigned piece of a State, the individuals of which will at that point be in disobedience to the United States will be at that point, thenceforward, and everlastingly free; and the official legislature of the United States, including the military and maritime authority thereof, will perceive and keep up the opportunity of such people, and will do no demonstration or acts to stifle such people, or any of them, in any endeavors they may make for their genuine opportunity."

The Proclamation denoted a momentous change in the government's situation on subjugation: up to that time, the government never had at any point taken a constrained master liberation position (and it could just do so now as a result of the 1861 flight of practically the entirety of the Southern individuals from Congress). However, its application was more restricted than the first shows up. It absolved the outskirt conditions of Delaware, Kentucky, Maryland, Missouri, and the new territory of West Virginia, and it likewise excluded those restricted segments of individual states which were faithful to the Union, for example, Virginia; in those states, servitude stayed legitimate until the confirmation of the Thirteenth Amendment in December 1865. Lincoln accepted that the government didn't have the position to preclude subjection; that would abuse states' privileges. As it may, he was additionally Commander of the Armed Forces. An activity against countries which were in the resistance, a stage towards their destruction, was utterly suitable. The South deciphered it as an unfriendly demonstration. This permitted Lincoln to disallow subjugation to a restricted degree, without touching off obstruction from hostile to abolitionist powers in the Union. No one of those slaves who lived outside the outskirt regions was quickly influenced, and it was the attacking Northern armed forces which upheld the denial.

While by and by contradicted to servitude, Lincoln accepted that the Constitution didn't enable Congress to end it, expressing in his First Inaugural Address that he "had no issue with [this] being made express and unavoidable" employing the Corwin Amendment. On social and political rights for blacks and africans, Lincoln expressed, "I am not, nor ever have been agreeable to making voters or members of the jury of negroes, nor of qualifying them to hold office, nor to intermarry with white individuals, I as much as any man am supportive of the better position doled out than the white race." The Emancipation Proclamation didn't make a difference to territories which were faithful to or constrained by, the Union. Subjection was not annulled in the U.S. until the entry of the thirteenth Amendment which was pronounced sanctioned on December 6, 1865.

Around 4,000,000 dark slaves were liberated in 1865. Ninety-five per cent of blacks lived in the South, containing 33% of its all-out populace. Conversely, just five per cent of blacks lived in the North, including only a single per cent of its entire people. Subsequently, fears of possible liberation were a lot more noteworthy in the South than in the North. In light of 1860 evaluation figures, 8% of guys who were matured 13 to 43 kicked the bucket in the conventional war, incorporating 6% in the North and 18% in the South. The horde style lynching of Will James, Cairo, Illinois, 1909. A horde of thousands watched the lynching.

After the Civil War, the thirteenth amendment in 1865, officially abolishing subjection, was endorsed. Moreover, Congress passed the Civil Rights Act of 1866, which expanded the scope of social liberties to all people conceived in the United States. Despite this, the rise of "Dark Codes", authorized demonstrations of oppression against blacks, kept on banning African-Americans from due social liberties. The Naturalization Act of 1790 restricted U.S. citizenship to whites just, and in 1868 the exertion toward social freedoms was underscored with the fourteenth amendment, which allowed citizenship to blacks. The Civil Rights Act of 1875 which was dispensed with in a choice that sabotaged government capacity to obstruct private racial separation. Regardless, the remainder of the Reconstruction Era alterations, the fifteenth amendment guaranteed to cast a ballot right to African-American men (already just white men of property could cast a ballot), and these total government endeavors, African-Americans started exploiting emancipation. African-Americans started casting a vote, looking for office positions, using government-funded instruction.

Before the finish of Reconstruction in the mid-1870s, vicious racial oppressors came to control utilizing paramilitary gatherings, for example, the Red Shirts and the White League and forced Jim Crow laws which denied African-Americans of casting ballot rights by establishing fundamental and prejudicial approaches of inconsistent racial isolation. Isolation, which started with subjection, proceeded with the entry and requirement of Jim Crow laws, alongside the posting of signs which were utilized to show blacks where they could lawfully walk, talk, drink, rest, or eat. For those spots that were racially blended, non-whites needed to hold up until every white client were managed. Private offices reached out from just white schools to white only burial grounds.

Local Americans

Local Americans have lived on the North American landmass for in any event 10,000 years, and a large number of Native Americans were living in what is today the United States at the time European pilgrims initially showed up. During the pilgrim and free periods, European pioneers pursued a great arrangement of contentions, regularly with the target of acquiring the assets of Native Americans. Through wars, constrained removal, (for example, the Trail of Tears), and the inconvenience of bargains, the land was taken. The loss of property frequently brought about hardships for Native Americans. In the mid-eighteenth century, the English had oppressed about 800 Choctaws.

After the production of the United States, the possibility of Indian evacuation picked up force. In any case, some Native Americans picked or were permitted to remain and evaded evacuation where after they were exposed to legitimate racism. The Choctaws in Mississippi depicted their circumstance in 1849, "we have had our homes torn down and consumed, our wall devastated, dairy cattle transformed into our fields and we have been scourged, manacled, shackled and in any case mishandled, until by such treatment a portion of our best men has kicked the bucket." Joseph B. Cobb, who moved to Mississippi, depicted the Choctaws as having "no respectability or righteousness by any means." In some regard, he discovered blacks, particularly local Africans, to be all the more intriguing and praiseworthy, the red man's boss all around. The Choctaw and Chickasaw, the clans he knew best, were underneath hatred, that is, surprisingly more terrible than dark slaves.

During the 1800s, belief systems, for example, Manifest predetermination, which held the view that the United States was bound to grow across the nation on the North American mainland, powered U.S. assaults against, and abuse of, Native Americans. In the years paving the way to the Indian Removal Act of 1830, there were many furnished clashes among pioneers and Native Americans. A defence for the success and oppression of indigenous individuals radiated from the generalized observation that Native Americans were "coldblooded Indian savages" (as portrayed in the United States Declaration of

Independence). Sam Wolfson in The Guardian expresses, "The affirmation's entry has regularly been referred to as an embodiment of the dehumanizing disposition toward indigenous Americans that the US was established on." Simon Moya-Smith, the culture supervisor at Indian Country Today, expresses, "Any occasion that would allude to my kin in such a repulsive, supremacist way is not worth celebrating. [July Fourth] is a day when we commend our strength, our way of life, our dialects, our kids and we grieve the millions – truly millions – of indigenous individuals who have kicked the bucket as a result of American colonialism."

In Martin Luther King Jr's. the book Why We Can't-Wait, he expressed, "Our country was conceived in destruction when it grasped the principle that the first American, the Indian, was a second rate race." In 1861, inhabitants of Mankato, Minnesota, framed the Knights of the Forest, with the objective of 'wiping out all Indians from Minnesota.' A grievous endeavor happened with the California dash for unheard of wealth, the initial two years of which saw the demise of thousands of Native Americans. Under Mexican standard in California, Indians were exposed to actual subjugation under an arrangement of peonage by the white world-class. While in 1850, California officially entered the Union as a free state, regarding the issue of bondage, the act of Indian obligated subjugation was not banned by the California Legislature until 1863. The 1864 expelling of the Navajos by the U.S. government happened when 8,000 Navajos were coercively moved to an internment camp in Bosque Redondo, where, under outfitted gatekeepers, more than 3,500 Navajo and Mescalero Apache men, ladies, and youngsters passed on from starvation and infection.

Local American countries on the fields in the west proceeded with equipped clashes with the U.S. all through the nineteenth century, through what was called commonly Indian Wars. Remarkable encounters in this period incorporate the Dakota War, Great Sioux War, Snake War and Colorado War. In the years paving the way to the Wounded Knee slaughter, the U.S. government had kept on holding onto Lakota lands. A Ghost Dance custom on the Northern Lakota reservation at Wounded Knee, South Dakota, prompted the U.S. Armed force's endeavor to stifle the Lakota. The move was a piece of a religion established by Wovoka that recounted the arrival of the Messiah to ease the enduring of Native Americans and guaranteed that if they would live equitable lives and play out the Ghost Dance appropriately, the European American trespassers would disappear, the buffalo would return, and the living and the dead would be brought together in an Edenic world. On 29th December 1890, at Wounded Knee, gunfire emitted, and U.S. fighters murdered up to 300 Indians, for the most part, elderly people men, ladies and youngsters.

During the period encompassing the 1890 Wounded Knee Massacre, creator L. Straight to the point Baum composed two articles about Americans. Five days after the murder of the

Lakota Sioux heavenly man, Sitting Bull, Baum expressed, "The glad soul of the first proprietors of these huge grasslands acquired through hundreds of years of wild and wicked wars for their ownership, waited toward the end in the chest of Sitting Bull. With his fall, the honorability of the Redskin is quenched, and what not many are left are a pack of whimpering mongrels who lick the hand that smites them. The Whites, by the law of triumph, by the equity of human progress, are experts of the American mainland, and the best wellbeing of the outskirts settlements will be made sure about by the complete demolition of a couple of outstanding Indians. Why not demolition? Their greatness has fled, their soul is broken, their masculinity destroyed; preferred that they bite the dust over live the hopeless blackguards that they are." Following the December 29, 1890, slaughter, Baum stated, "The Pioneer has before pronounced that our lone security relies on the all-out annihilation [sic] of the Indians. Having wronged them for a given period of time we would do well too, to ensure our development, tail it up by one all the more off-base and wipe these untamed and wild animals from the substance of the earth. In this falsehoods wellbeing for our pioneers and the troopers who are under awkward orders. Else, we may anticipate that future years should be as brimming with an issue with the redskins as those have been previously."

Military and common obstruction by Native Americans has been a steady component of American history. So to have an assortment of discussions around issues of sway, the maintaining of arrangement arrangements, and the social equality of Native Americans under U.S. law.

Reservation minimization

When their regions were joined into the United States, enduring Native Americans were denied fairness under the steady gaze of the law and frequently rewarded as dependents of the government.

Numerous Native Americans were moved to reservations— establishing 4% of U.S. domain. In various cases, bargains marked with Native Americans were abused. A considerable number of American Indians and Alaska Natives had to go to a private educational system which looked to re-teach them in white pilgrim American qualities, culture and economy.

The Nazis respected the treatment of Native Americans. Nazi extension eastbound was gone with the summoning of America's rural development westbound under the standard of Manifest Destiny, with the going with wars on the Native Americans. In 1928, Hitler lauded Americans for having "gunned down a large number of Redskins to two or three hundred thousand and now hold the unassuming remainder under perception in pen". On Nazi Germany's extension eastbound, Hitler expressed, "Our Mississippi must be the Volga and not the Niger."

Further dispossession of different sorts proceeds into the present. However, these present dispossessions, particularly regarding land, once in a while make significant news features in the nation (e.g., the Lenape individuals' ongoing monetary difficulties and ensuing area get by the State of New Jersey), and now and then even neglect to cause it to features in the territories in which they to happen. Through concessions for businesses, for example, oil, mining and wood and through the division of land from the Allotment Act, these concessions have raised issues of consent, misuse of low sovereignty rates, ecological foul play, and gross botch of assets held in trust, bringing about the loss of $10–40 billion. The World watch Institute takes note of that 317 reservations are undermined by ecological dangers, while Western Shoshone land has been exposed to more than 1,000 atomic blasts.

Digestion

The legislature selected specialists, similar to Benjamin Hawkins, to live among the Native Americans and to show them, through model and guidance, how to live like whites. America's first president, George Washington, detailed an arrangement to energize the "enlightening" process.

The Naturalization Act of 1790s restricted citizenship to whites as it were. The Indian Citizenship Act of 1924 conceded U.S. citizenship to every Native American. Before the entry of the demonstration, about 66% of Native Americans were at that point U.S. residents. The most accurate recorded date of Native Americans turning out to be U.S. residents was in 1831 when the Mississippi Choctaw became residents after the United States Legislature approved the Treaty of Dancing Rabbit Creek. Under article XIV of that bargain, any Choctaw who chose not to move to Native American Territory could turn into an American resident when he enlisted and on the off chance that he remained on assigned grounds for a long time after arrangement endorsement.

While formal balance has been lawfully perceived, American Indians, Alaska Natives, Native Hawaiians, and Pacific Islanders stay among the most financially impeded gatherings in the nation, and as per National emotional well-being contemplates, American Indians as a gathering will in general experience the ill effects of significant levels of liquor abuse, discouragement and self-destruction.

Hostile to Chinese enactment

The 1879 Act of the State of California restricted the work of Chinese individuals by state and neighborhood governments, just as by organizations that were fused in California. Likewise, the 1879 California constitution appointed capacity to nearby administrations of California to expel Chinese individuals from inside their fringes. The Chinese Exclusion Act forbidding the migration of Chinese workers was instituted on the national level in 1882. A few slaughter of Chinese individuals, including the Rock Springs slaughter of 1885 and the Hells Canyon slaughter of 1887 further exemplified profound American supremacist hostility against Chinese individuals.

Post-Reconstruction Era

African dwarf Ota Benga, human display, at the Bronx Zoo, New York in 1906. Displayed in the zoo's Monkey House, dark priests fought to zoo authorities. James H. Gordon, "Our race, we believe, is sufficiently discouraged, without displaying one of us with the chimps. We think we are deserving of being viewed as people, with spirits."

The new century saw a solidifying of regulated racism and lawful victimization residents of African plummet in the United States. All through the post Civil War period, racial separation was casually and foundationally implemented, to set the previous social request. Even though they were, in fact, ready to cast a ballot, survey charges, inescapable demonstrations of psychological warfare, for example, lynchings (frequently executed by despising gatherings, for example, the renewed Ku Klux Klan, established in the Reconstruction South), and biased laws, for instance, granddad statements kept dark Americans (and numerous Poor Whites) disappointed especially in the South. Moreover, segregation stretched out to state enactment that "designated incomprehensibly inconsistent monetary help" for profoundly different schools. Furthermore, province authorities here and there redistributed assets which were reserved for blacks to white schools, further subverting instructive chances. In light of by right racism, dissent and lobbyist bunches rose, most eminently, the NAACP

This timespan is some of the time alluded to as the nadir of American race relations since racism, isolation, racial segregation, and articulations of racial domination all expanded. So did enemy of dark brutality, including race uproars, for example, the Atlanta Race mob of 1906 and the Tulsa race mob of 1921. The Atlanta revolt was described by the French paper Le Petit Journal as a "racial slaughter of negroes". The Charleston News and Courier wrote in light of the Atlanta riots: "Division of the races is the main radical arrangement of the negro issue in this nation. Nothing is surprising about it. It was the Almighty who built up the limits of the home of the races. The negroes were brought here by impulse; they ought to be actuated to leave here by influence."

The Great Migration

Moreover, racism, which had been seen primarily as an issue in the Southern states, burst onto the national cognizance following the Great Migration, the movement of a considerable number of African Americans from their foundations in the rustic Southern states to the cold places of the North and West somewhere in the range of 1910 and 1970, especially in urban areas, for example, Boston, Chicago, New York City (Harlem), Los Angeles and Oakland and Seattle, Portland and Phoenix, and Denver. Inside Chicago, for instance, somewhere in the range of 1910 and 1970, the level of African-Americans jumped from 2.0 per cent to 32.7 per cent. The segment examples of dark vagrants and outside financial conditions are, to a great extent, contemplated energizer to the Great Migration. For instance, moving blacks (somewhere in the range of 1910 and 1920) were more prone to be proficient than blacks that stayed in the South. Realized monetary push factors assumed a job in relocation, for example, the rise of a split work advertise and rural misery from the boll weevil annihilation of the cotton economy.

Southern transients were regularly rewarded as per previous racial definition. The quick deluge of blacks into the North and West upset the racial parity inside urban communities, compounding threatening vibe between both high contrast occupants in the two districts. Stereotypic constructions of

Southern blacks were utilized to quality issues in urban regions, for example, wrongdoing and ailment, to the nearness of African-Americans. In general, African-Americans in generally Northern and Western urban communities experienced foundational segregation in plenty of parts of life. Inside work, monetary open doors for blacks were directed to the most minimal status and prohibitive in potential versatility. Inside the lodging market, more grounded unfair measures were utilized in connection to the convergence, bringing about a blend of "focused viciousness, prohibitive agreements, redlining and racial guiding".

All through this period, racial pressures detonated, most savagely in Chicago, and lynchings—horde coordinated hangings, usually racially propelled—expanded drastically during the 1920s. Urban mobs—whites assaulting blacks—turned into a northern and western issue. Many whites shielded their space with savagery, terrorizing, or legitimate strategies toward African Americans. In contrast, many different whites moved to all the more racially homogeneous rural or exurban locales, a procedure known as white flight. Racially prohibitive lodging contracts were controlled unenforceable under the Fourteenth Amendment in the 1948 milestone Supreme Court case Shelley v. Kraemer.

Chosen in 1912, President Woodrow Wilson requested isolation all through the government. In World War I, blacks served with passion in the US Armed Forces in isolated units. Dark officers were regularly inadequately prepared and prepared and were frequently put on the bleeding edges in self-destruction missions. The U.S. military was still vigorously isolated in World War II. What's more, no African-American would get the Medal of Honor during the war, and dark troopers needed to some of the time surrender their seats in trains to the Nazi detainees of war.

World War II to the Civil Rights EraThe Jim Crow Laws were state and neighborhood laws established in the Southern and outskirt conditions of the United States and upheld somewhere in the range of 1876 and 1965. They commanded "separate however equivalent" status for blacks. In all actuality, this prompted treatment and facilities that were quite often substandard compared to those who were given to whites. The most significant laws necessitated that government-funded schools, open spots and accessible transportation, similar to trains and transports, have separate offices for whites and blacks. State-supported school isolation was proclaimed unlawful by the Supreme Court of the United States in 1954 in Brown v. Leading group of Education. One of the central government legal disputes which tested isolation in schools was Mendez v. Westminster in 1946.

During the 1950, the Civil Rights Movement was picking up force. Participation in the NAACP expanded in states over the

U.S. A 1955 lynching that started open shock about bad form was that of Emmett Till, a 14-year-old kid from Chicago. Going through the mid-year with his family members in Money, Mississippi, Till was murdered for supposedly having wolf-whistled at a white lady. Till had been gravely beaten, one of his eyes was gouged out, and he was shot in the head before being tossed into the Tallahatchie River, his body overloaded with a 70-pound cotton gin fan tied strongly around his neck with spiked metal. David Jackson composes that Mamie Till, Emmett's Mother, "brought him home to Chicago and demanded an open coffin. Several thousand recorded past Till's remaining parts. Yet, it was the distribution of the singing memorial service picture in Jet, with an apathetic Mamie looking at her killed youngster's assaulted body, that constrained the world to deal with the ruthlessness of American racism." News photos flowed around the nation and drew an extraordinary open response. The instinctive reaction to his mom's choice to have an open-coffin memorial service activated the dark network all through the U.S. Vann R. Newkirk expressed "the preliminary of his executioners turned into an exhibition lighting up the oppression of racial oppression". The territory of Mississippi attempted two litigants, Roy Bryant and J.W. Milam,

however, they were rapidly vindicated by an all-white jury.

In light of increasing separation and brutality, peaceful demonstrations of dissent started to happen. For instance, in February 1960, in Greensboro, North Carolina, four youthful African-American undergrads entered a Woolworth store and took a seat at the counter yet were denied assistance. The men had found out about peaceful dissent in school, and kept on sitting calmly as whites tormented them at the table, pouring ketchup on their heads and consuming them with cigarettes. After this, many demonstrations occurred to challenge racism and imbalance peacefully. Protests proceeded all through the South and spread to different zones. In the long run, after many events and other peaceful fights, including walks and blacklists, places started to consent to integrate.

In June 1963, social equality dissident and NAACP part Medgar Evers were killed by Byron De La Beckwith, an individual from the White Citizens' Council. In his preliminaries for homicide De La Beckwith sidestepped conviction through every single white jury (the two preliminaries finished with hung juries).

The Sixteenth Street Baptist Church besieging denoted a defining moment during the Civil Rights Era. On Sunday, September 15, 1963, with a heap of explosive covered up on an outside flight of stairs, Ku Klux Klansmen decimated one side of the Birmingham church. The bomb detonated in closeness to twenty-six youngsters who were getting ready for ensemble practice in the cellar gathering room. The blast executed four dark young ladies, Carole Robertson (14), Cynthia Wesley (14), Denise McNair (11) and Addie Mae Collins (14).

With the shelling happening just two or three weeks after Martin Luther King Jr's. March on Washington for Jobs and Freedom of living, it turned into a necessary part of the changed impression of conditions for blacks in America. It impacted the section of the Civil Rights Act of 1964 (that restricted separation in open housing, work, and worker's guilds) and Voting Rights Act of 1965, which overruled remaining Jim Crow laws. In any case, neither had been actualized before the finish of the 1960s as social liberties pioneers kept on taking a stab at the political and social opportunity.

Numerous U.S. states restricted interracial marriage. In 1967, Mildred Loving, a dark lady, and Richard Loving, a white man, were condemned to a year in jail in Virginia for wedding one another. Their marriage abused the state's enemy of miscegenation rule, the Racial Integrity Act of 1924, which denied marriage between individuals delegated white and individuals named "shaded" (people of the non-white family line). In the Loving v. Virginia case in the mid-1967, the Supreme Court nullified laws precluding interracial marriage in the U.S.

Isolation proceeded much after the downfall of the Jim Crow laws. Information on house costs and mentalities towards reconciliation propose that in the mid-twentieth century, segregation was a result of aggregate activities taken by whites to prohibit blacks from their neighborhoods. Isolation additionally appeared as redlining, the act of denying or expanding the expense of administrations, for example, banking, protection, access to occupations, access to medicinal services, or even general stores to occupants in particular, regularly racially decided, zones. Although in the U.S., casual separation and isolation have consistently existed, redlining started with the National Housing Act of 1934, which built up the Federal Housing Administration (FHA). The training was battled first through a section of the Fair Housing Act of 1968 (which forestalls redlining when the models for redlining depend on race, religion, sexual orientation, familial status, incapacity, or ethnic starting point), and later through the Community Reinvestment Act of 1977, which expects banks to apply similar loaning rules in all networks. Although redlining is unlawful, some contend that it keeps on existing in different structures.

Up until the 1940s, the full income capability of what was designated "the Negro market" was to a great extent overlooked by white-claimed makers in the U.S. with promoting concentrated on whites. Blacks were additionally denied business bargains. On his choice to participate in display races against racehorses to acquire cash, Olympic victor Jesse Owens expressed, "Individuals state that it was corrupting for an Olympic hero to run against a pony, however, what was I expected to do? I had four gold decorations, yet you can't eat four gold awards." On the absence of chances, Owens included, "There was no TV, no large publicizing, no supports at that point. Not for a dark man, in any case." In the gathering to respect his Olympic achievement Owens was not allowed to enter through the principle entryways of the Waldorf Astoria New York and instead compelled to venture out up to the occasion in a cargo lift. The primary dark Academy Award beneficiary Hattie McDaniel was not allowed to go to the debut of gone with the Wind with Georgia being isolated racially, and at the Oscars function in LA she was required to sit at a separate table at the furthest mass of the room; the inn had a severe no-blacks arrangement, however, permitted McDaniel in the act of goodwill some help.

As the social equality development and the destroying of Jim Crow laws during the 1950s and 1960s extended existing racial strains in a significant part of the Southern U.S, a Republican Party discretionary technique – the Southern procedure – was sanctioned to increment political help among white voters in the South by engaging racism against African Americans. Republican government officials, for example, presidential applicant Richard Nixon and Representative Barry Goldwater created systems that effectively added to the political realignment of many white, preservationist voters in the South who had customarily bolstered the Democratic Party as opposed to the Republican Party. In 1971, enraged by African representatives at the UN disagreeing with the U.S. in a vote, at that point Governor of California Ronald Reagan expressed in a call to President Nixon, "To see those... monkeys from those African nations - damn them, they're as yet awkward wearing shoes!" The recognition that the Republican Party had filled in as the "vehicle of racial oppression in the South", especially post 1964, made it hard for the Party to win back the help of dark voters in the South in later years.

The 1980s to the present

While generous increases were made in the succeeding a long time through white-collar class progression and open business, deep poverty and absence of instruction proceeded with regards to de-industrialization. Despite increases made after the sixteenth Street Baptist Church shelling, some viciousness against dark houses of worship has additionally moved – 145 discharge was set to places of worship around the South during the 1990s, and a mass shooting in Charleston, South Carolina was submitted in 2015 at the noteworthy Mother Emanuel Church.

From 1981 to 1997, the US Department of Agriculture victimized a considerable number of dark American ranchers, denying advances that were given to white ranchers in similar conditions. The separation was the subject of the Pigford v. Glickman claim brought by individuals from the National Black Farmers Association, which brought about two settlement understandings of $1.25 billion out of 1999 and $1.15 billion out of 2009.

During the 1980s and '90s, various mobs happened that were identified with longstanding racial pressures among police and minority networks. The 1980 Miami riots were analyzed by the murdering of an African-American driver by four white Miami-Dade Police officials. They were in this manner cleared on charges of homicide and proof altering. Thus, the six-day 1992 Los Angeles riots ejected after the absolution of four white LAPD officials who had been recorded beating Rodney King, an African-American driver. Khalil Gibran, the Director of the Harlem-based Schomburg Center for Research in Black Culture, has distinguished more than 100 cases of mass racial savagery in the United States since 1935 and has noticed that pretty much every case was hastened by a police occurrence.

Strategically, the "champ take-all" structure that applies to 48 out of 50 states in the constituent school benefits white portrayal, as no country has voters of shading as most of the electorate. This has been depicted as auxiliary inclination and frequently directs voters of shading to feel politically estranged, and in this way not to cast a ballot. The absence of portrayal in Congress has additionally prompted lower voter turnout. Starting in 2016, African Americans just made up 8.7% of Congress, and Latinos 7%.

Many refer to the 2008 United States presidential political race as a stage forward in race relations: white Americans assumed a job in choosing Barack Obama, the nation's first dark president. Obama got a more prominent level of the white vote (43%), than did the past Democratic up-and-comer, John Kerry (41%). Racial divisions persevered all through the political decision; wide edges of Black voters gave Obama an advantage during the presidential essential, where 8 out of 10 African-Americans decided in favour of him in the primaries, and an MSNBC survey found that race was a critical factor in whether an applicant was seen as being prepared for office. In South Carolina, "Whites were far likelier to name Clinton than Obama as being generally able to be president, likeliest to join the nation and generally adept at catching the White House in November. Blacks named Obama over Clinton by much more grounded edges—two-and three-to-one—in every one of the three regions."

Humanist Russ Long expressed in 2013 that there is currently increasingly inconspicuous racism that connects a particular race with a specific trademark. In a recent report directed by Katz and Braly, it was introduced that "blacks and whites hold an assortment of generalizations towards one another, frequently negative". The Katz and Braley concentrate additionally found that African-Americans and whites see the attributes that they distinguish each other with as compromising, interracial correspondence between the two is probably going to be "reluctant, held, and hiding". Generalizations guide interracial mail; generalizations are moved into character and character characteristics which at that point affect correspondence. Different elements go into how generalizations are set up, for example, age and the setting in which they are being applied. For instance, in an investigation done by the Entman-Rojecki Index of Race and Media in 2014, 89% of dark ladies in films are indicated swearing and showing hostile conduct while just 17% of white ladies are depicted as such.

In 2012, Trayvon Martin, a seventeen-year-old young person, was lethally shot by George Zimmerman in Sanford, Florida. Zimmerman, an area watch volunteer, guaranteed that Martin was being dubious and called the Sanford police to report him. Between closure his call with police and their appearance, Zimmerman lethally shot Martin outside of the apartment he was remaining at following a fight. Zimmerman was harmed in the battle and guaranteed self-protection. The occurrence caused national shock after Zimmerman was not charged over the shooting. The civic inclusion of the event lead Sandford police to capture Zimmerman and accuse him of second-degree murder, yet he was seen not as liable at preliminary. Open clamour followed the quittance and made an abundance of doubt among minorities and the Sanford police.

In 2014, the police killing of Michael Brown, an African American, in Ferguson, Missouri led to significant turmoil in the town. In the years following, broad communications have accompanied other prominent police shootings of African-Americans, frequently with video proof from police body-worn cameras. Among 15 notable police shooting passings of African-Americans, just one official confronted jail time. Prominent shooting passings of African-Americans lead to the making of the Black Lives Matter development.

The U.S. Equity division propelled the National Center for Building Community Trust and Justice in 2014. This program gathers information concerning racial profiling to make a change in the criminal equity framework concerning specific and unequivocal racial predisposition towards African-Americans just as different minorities.

In August 2017, the UNCERD (UN Committee on the Elimination of Racial Discrimination) gave an uncommon warning to the US and its initiative to "unequivocally and genuinely" censure bigot discourse and wrongdoing, following viciousness in Charlottesville during a convention composed by white patriots, racial oppressors, Klansmen, neo-Nazis and different conservative civilian armies in July.

White ladies calling the police on blacks has gotten increasingly plugged lately. In a recent 2020 article in The New York Times, How White Women Use Themselves as Instruments of Terror, dark reporter Charles M. Blow stated, "verifiably, white ladies have utilized the savagery of white men and the foundations these men control as their muscle. Untold quantities of lynchings were executed because white ladies had asserted that a dark man assaulted, ambushed, conversed with or looked at them. This activity in racial radicalism has been hauled into the cutting edge period through the weaponizing of 9-1-1, regularly by white ladies, to summon the force and power of the police who they are completely mindful are antagonistic to dark men". One such model that became a web sensation happened in May 2020, when a white lady called the police on a dark man winged animal viewing in Central Park, New York. After he had requested that she put her pooch on a rope (according to the standards in a region of the recreation centre to secure other untamed life), she moved toward him, to which he reacted "Kindly don't approach me", before she hollered, "I'm snapping a photo and calling the cops. I'm going to let them know an African American man is undermining my life." During her call, with the man stood a good ways from her and recording her, she talked in a perceptibly distressed voice, "There's a man, African American, he is.. compromising me and my canine. If it's not trouble send the cops right away!". Different instances of white ladies calling the police on blacks incorporate, announcing an eight-year-old young lady for selling jugs of water without a grant in San Francisco, detailing a dark family grilling in a recreation centre in Oakland, California, obstructing a mysterious man from entering a high rise in St. Louis, Missouri where he is an inhabitant before calling the police, and a lady blaming a kid for grabbing her in a store in Brooklyn, New York which was disproven by reconnaissance.

On May 25, 2020, George Floyd, was killed by a white Minneapolis Police Department official, Derek Chauvin, who constrained his knee on Floyd's neck for an aggregate of 8 minutes and 46 seconds. Each of the four cops presents was terminated the following day. Floyd's passing started a rush of quiet and savage fights over the US, starting in Minneapolis. The official after death report on June 1, 2020, affirmed that the demise was manslaughter.

Contemporary issues

Hate issues and killing

In the United States, most wrongdoings in which casualties are focused based on their race or ethnicity are viewed as abhor violations. (For government law purposes, wrongdoings in which Hispanics are concentrated on due to their personality are seen as hating violations dependent on ethnicity.) Leading types of predisposition which are referred to in the FBI's Uniform Crime Reporting (UCR) Program, in light of law implementation office filings include: against a dark, hostile to Jewish, hostile to white, against gay, and Hispanic inclination in a specific order in both 2004 and 2005. As indicated by the Bureau of Justice Measurements, whites, blacks, and Hispanics had comparative paces of brutal loathe wrongdoing exploitation somewhere in the range of 2007 and 2011. Notwithstanding, from 2011 to 2012, brutal despise wrongdoings against Hispanic individuals expanded by 300%. While thinking about all hate violations, not merely rough ones, African Americans are bound to be casualties than other racial gatherings.

The New Century Foundation, a white patriot association established by Jared Taylor, contends that blacks are bound to carry out detest violations than whites, and it additionally contends that FBI figures blow up the quantity of abhorring wrongdoings submitted by whites by considering Hispanics "white". Different investigators are forcefully incredulous of the NCF's discoveries, alluding to the standard criminological view that "Racial and ethnic information must be treated with alert. Existing exploration on wrongdoing has, by and large, demonstrated that racial or ethnic character isn't cautious of criminal conduct with information which has been controlled for social and financial variables." NCF's system and measurements are further strongly condemned as defective and beguiling by against bigot activists Tim Wise and the Southern Law Center.

The central post-Jim Crow time detest wrongdoing to make hair-raising media consideration was the homicide of Vincent Chin, an Asian American of Chinese plummet in 1982. He was assaulted by two white aggressors who were as of late laid off from a Detroit territory auto processing plant work and criticized the Japanese for their joblessness. Jawline was not of Japanese plummet. However, the attackers affirmed in the criminal legal dispute that he "resembled a Jap". This ethnic slur is utilized to depict Japanese and different Asians, and they were sufficiently irate to pound the life out of him.

Contemptuous perspectives

Proceeding with discrimination against Jews in the United States has stayed an issue and the 2011 Survey of American Behavior Toward Jews in America, discharged by the Anti-Defamation League (ADL), has discovered that the ongoing scene monetary downturn expanded the declaration of some racist perspectives among Americans. The majority of the people who were reviewed communicated genius Jewish conclusions, with 64% of them concurring that Jews have contributed a lot to U.S. social culture. However, the surveying likewise found that 19% of Americans addressed "most likely obvious" to the extreme canard that "Jews have an excessive amount of control/impact on Wall Street". In comparison, 15% of Americans agreed with the related proclamation that Jews appear "additionally ready to utilize obscure practices" in business than others do. Thinking about the waiting discrimination against Jews of around one of every five Americans, Abraham H. Foxman, the ADL's national executive, has contended, "It is upsetting that with the entirety of the steps we have made in turning into a progressively open-minded society, hostile to Semitic convictions keep on holding a bad habit grasp on a little however not deficient fragment of the American open."

An ABC News report in 2007 described that past ABC surveys over quite a long while have would, in general, locate that "six per cent have self-announced harbouring a bias against Jews, 27 per cent have self-revealed harbouring partiality against Muslims, 25 per cent have self-detailed harbouring preference against Arabs," and "one out of 10 have surrendered harbouring, in any event, a smidgen of bias " against Hispanic Americans. The report additionally expressed that a full 34% of Americans revealed harbouring "some bigot sentiments" by and large as a self-portrayal. An Associated Press and Yahoo News overview of 2,227 grown-up Americans in 2008 found that 10% of white respondents expressed that "a great deal" of separation despite everything exists against African-Americans while 45% of white respondents expressed that lone "a few" segregation despite everything exists against African Americans contrasted with 57% of dark respondents who revealed that "a ton" of separation despite everything exists against African Americans. In a similar survey, more whites applied positive credits to coloured Americans than negative ones, with blacks depicting whites considerably more profoundly, however a noteworthy minority of whites despite everything called African Americans "flippant", "apathetic", or other such things.

In 2008, Stanford University political specialist Paul Sniderman commented that in the cutting edge U.S., racism and partialities are "a profound test, and it's one that Americans by and large, and besides, political researchers, simply haven't been prepared to recognize completely."

In 2017, residents assembled in the school network of Charlottesville, Virginia to go to the Unite the Right meeting. One lady was executed, and many others were harmed when a racial oppressor drove his vehicle into a gathering of counter-dissidents. VP Mike Pence criticized the brutality expressing, "We have no resilience for abhorring and savagery from racial oppressors, neo-Nazis or the KKK. These hazardous periphery bunches have no spot in American open life and the American discussion, and we blame them in the most grounded potential terms."

Mitigation

There is extensive plenty of cultural and political proposals to reduce the impacts of proceeded with separation in the United States. For instance, inside colleges, it has been proposed that a sort of advisory group could react to non-sanctionable conduct.

It is likewise contended that there is a requirement for "white understudies and staff to reformulate white-mindfulness toward a progressively secure character that isn't compromised by dark social foundations and that can perceive the racial non-lack of bias of the establishment's whites overwhelm" (Brown, 334). Matched with this exertion, Brown empowers the expansion in minority employees, so the implanted white regulating experience starts to part.

Inside the media, it is discovered that racial signals prime racial stereotypic idea. In this manner, it is contended that "generalization conflicting prompts may prompt more intentioned thought, subsequently stifling racial preparing impacts." Social analysts, for example, Jennifer Eberhardt, have accomplished work that shows such preparing impacts subliminally help decide perspectives and conduct toward people paying little heed to goals. These outcomes have been consolidated into preparing, for instance, in some police divisions.

It has likewise been contended that more proof-based direction from clinicians and sociologists is required with the end goal for individuals to realize what is compelling in lightening racism. Such proof-based methodologies can uncover, for instance, the various mental inclinations to which people are subject, for example, ingroup predisposition and the major attribution blunder, which can underlie bigot perspectives.

Clinician Stuart Vyse has contended that contention, thoughts, and realities won't patch divisions. Yet, there is proof, for example, that which is given by the Robbers Cave Experiment, that looking for shared objectives can help ease racism.

Murdering of George Floyd

On May 25, 2020, George Floyd, kicked the bucket bound behind his back and inclined on a Minneapolis, Minnesota road, while white cop Derek Chauvin bowed on his neck for just about nine minutes. Two different officials further controlled Floyd, who had been captured on doubt of utilizing a fake bill, and a fourth kept spectators from interceding as Floyd asked for his life and over and again said: "I can't relax". During the last three minutes, Floyd was still and had no heartbeat. Yet, the officials overlooked spectators' supplications that Chauvin expels his knee from Floyd's neck, which he didn't do even as showing up doctors endeavored to treat Floyd.

Police at first guaranteed that Floyd had opposed capture, however, dealers' surveillance camera film and recordings made by witnesses negated that guarantee. Each of the four officials was terminated the day after Floyd's passing. Two post-mortem examinations saw Floyd's demise as a crime. Be that as it may, Minnesota Attorney General Keith Ellison updated the charges against Chauvin to second-degree death and charged the other three officials with helping and abetting second-degree murder.

Floyd's demise activated showings and fights in more than 75 U.S urban communities and around the globe against police severity, police racism, and absence of police responsibility.

Exhibitions in specific urban communities turned brutal, remembering for Atlanta, Chicago, Los Angeles, Minneapolis, New York City, Philadelphia, and Washington D.C. In the Minneapolis–Saint Paul territory, a police region and two stores were seared, and stores were plundered. A few demonstrators skirmished with police, who discharged nerve gas and elastic shots. There were additionally dissents in nations around the globe.

Floyd's demise has been contrasted with that of Eric Garner, a dark man who was executed in 2014 during capture for illegally selling cigarettes, and who – like Floyd – rehashed "I can't breathe" while a New York City cop applied a deadly stranglehold.

Individuals included

George Perry Floyd, age 46, was conceived in Fayetteville, North Carolina, and brought up in the Third Ward of Houston, Texas. In 2014, he moved to Minneapolis, Minnesota.

Derek Michael Chauvin, who was 44 years old, had been a cop in the Minneapolis Police Department since 2001. He had 18 protests on his official record, two of which brought about the order including formal letters of criticism. He had been associated with three official included shootings, one of them lethal. Chauvin was granted decorations of valour in 2006 and 2008 for episodes in which he terminated at suspects, and in

2008 and 2009 got recognitions for seeking after suspects. Floyd and Chauvin had worked covering shifts as security watches at a dance club, as per a previous club proprietor who was unsure whether Floyd and Chauvin knew one another. The former proprietor likewise said that Chauvin was now and then overaggressive in managing the club's for the most part dark customer base, for instance reacting to battles by splashing a whole group with mace as opposed to managing those battling.

Tou Thao, age 34, had been a cop in the Minneapolis Police Department. He began as low maintenance network administration official in 2008 and experienced the police institute in 2009. In the wake of being laid off for a long time, he continued working for the police in 2012. Six grumblings had been documented against Thao, none bringing about the disciplinary activity. In 2014, a man guaranteed Thao cuffed him without cause, tossed him to the ground, and punched him badly, kicked, and kneed him; the man's teeth were broken, and he was hospitalized. The subsequent claim was agreed to $25,000.

J. Alexander Kueng and Thomas K. Path, age 37, were authorized as law implementation officials in August 2019. Kueng and Lane were in their first seven day stretch of administration as Minneapolis cops when George Floyd was killed.

Capture and demise

On the night of Memorial Day, May 25, 2020, Floyd bought cigarettes at Cup Foods, a supermarket at the crossing point of East 38th Street and Chicago Avenue in the Powderhorn Park neighborhood of Minneapolis. A store worker trusted Floyd had paid with a fake $20 greenback.

Not long before 8:00 pm, two Cup Foods workers left the store and went across the road to an SUV left before an eatery; Floyd was in the driver's seat, and two different grown-ups were in the vehicle. The representatives requested that Floyd return the cigarettes, and he won't. The café's surveillance camera recorded the cooperation. At 8:01, a store representative called police to report that Floyd had passed "counterfeit bills" and was "dreadfully tanked" and "not in charge of himself".

At 8:08, Kueng and Lane showed up, quickly entering Cup Foods before going across the road to Floyd's SUV. The path took out his firearm and requested Floyd to put his hands on the controlling wheel; Floyd went along, and Lane holstered his weapon. Somebody stopped behind Floyd's SUV started recording a video at 8:10. Following a short battle, Lane pulled Floyd from the SUV and bound him. At 8:12, Kueng sat George Floyd on the walkway against the divider before the café. As indicated by criminal objections documented against the officials by state examiners, Floyd was "quiet" and said, "bless your heart".

Chauvin stoops on Floyd's neck.

At 8:13, Kueng and Lane revealed to Floyd he was set to be taken to jail and strolled him to their squad car over the road. Floyd tumbled to the ground close to the vehicle; the officials got him and put him against the vehicle's entryway. As indicated by investigators, Floyd told the officials that he was not opposing, yet that he was claustrophobic and would not like to sit in the vehicle. A Minneapolis Park Police officers showed up and protected Floyd's vehicle (over the road by the café) and the two individuals who had been in it with Floyd.

At 8:17, a third squad car showed up with officials Derek Michael Chauvin and Tou Thao, who joined Kueng and Lane. Chauvin accepted order. As per examiners, Floyd told the officials he was unable to inhale while they attempted to drive him into the vehicle. Around 8:18, security film from Cup Foods shows Kueng battling with Floyd for in any event a moment in the driver side rearward sitting arrangement while Thao watches. At 8:19, remaining on the traveller side of the vehicle, Chauvin pulled Floyd over the rearward sitting arrangement from the driver side to the traveller side, at that point out of the car. Floyd, still cuffed, tumbled to the asphalt where he lay on his chest with his cheek to the ground. Floyd quit moving around 8:20, however, he was as yet conscious.

Numerous observers started to film the experience; their recordings flowed broadly on the web. At 8:20, an observer over the road started recording video indicating Chauvin stooping on Floyd's neck, Kueng applying strain to Floyd's middle, and Lane applying tension to Floyd's legs, while Thao stood close by. This observer quit shooting when one of the officials requested him to leave. Likewise, at 8:20, a subsequent individual, remaining close to the passage of Cup Foods, started recording the occurrence. Floyd can be heard over and over saying "I can't breathe", "If you don't mind and "Mother"; Floyd rehashed, in any event, multiple times that he was unable to relax. At a certain point, an observer stated: "You got him down. Allow him to relax." After Floyd said, "I'm going to pass on", Chauvin advised him to "unwind". An official ask Floyd, "What do you need?"; Floyd replied, "I can't relax". Floyd states: "If it's not too much trouble the knee in my neck, I can't relax."

At around 8:22, the officials required a rescue vehicle on a non-crisis premise, raising the call to crisis status a moment later. Chauvin kept on bowing on Floyd's neck. A bystander hollered to Floyd, "Well, get up, get in the vehicle, man", Floyd, still bound and face down on the asphalt, reacted, "I can't", while Chauvin's knee stayed on his neck. Floyd shouted out "Mother!" twice. Floyd stated, "My stomach harms, my neck harms, everything harms", mentioned water, and asked, "Don't slaughter me." One observer called attention to that Floyd was seeping from the nose. Another told the officials that Floyd was "not in any event, opposing capture at present". Thao countered that George Floyd was "talking, he's fine"; an observer answered that Floyd "ain't fine. Get him off the ground ... You could have placed him in the vehicle at this point. He's not opposing capture or nothing. You're getting a charge out of it. Take a gander at you. Your non-verbal communication clarifies it." As Floyd kept on weeping for help, Thao said to witnesses: "This is the reason you don't take drugs, kids."

By 8:25, Floyd seemed oblivious, and observers defied the officials about Floyd's condition. Chauvin pulled out mace to fend onlookers off as Thao moved among them and Chauvin. Onlookers more than once shouted that Floyd was "not responsive at this moment" and encouraged the officials to check his heartbeat. Kueng checked Floyd's wrist yet discovered no heartbeat; the officials didn't endeavor to give Floyd clinical help. As indicated by the criminal grievance against Chauvin, Lane inquired as to whether they should move Floyd onto his side, and Chauvin said no. An observer asked, "Did they screwing execute him?"

Clinical reaction and demise
At 8:27 pm, a Hennepin County emergency vehicle showed up. Presently, a youthful relative of the proprietor of Cup Foods endeavored to mediate, however, was pushed back by Thao. Crisis clinical specialists checked Floyd's heartbeat. Chauvin saved his knee on Floyd's neck for nearly 60 seconds after the

rescue vehicle showed up, regardless of Floyd being quiet and unmoving. When he at long last lifted his knee, it had been there for eight minutes and forty-six seconds. Around 8:29, Floyd, still unmoving, was stacked into the rescue vehicle which left for Hennepin County Medical Center.

On the way, the rescue vehicle mentioned help from the Minneapolis Fire Department. At 8:32, firefighters showed up at Cup Foods; as per their report, the cops gave no unmistakable data in regards to Floyd's condition or whereabouts, which deferred their capacity to discover the rescue vehicle. In the interim, the emergency vehicle revealed that Floyd was entering heart failure and again mentioned help, requesting that firefighters meet them at the edge of 36th Street and Park Avenue. After five minutes, the local group of fire-fighters arrived at the emergency vehicle; two local groups of fire-fighters surgeons who boarded the rescue vehicle discovered Floyd lethargically and pulseless. Floyd was articulated dead at 9:25 at the Hennepin County Medical Center crisis room.

Examinations and criminal allegations

Police office reaction

On 26th May, the morning after Floyd was slaughtered, the Minneapolis Police Department gave an announcement asserting that Floyd had "truly opposed" and that after officials cuffed him, they "noted he seemed, by all accounts, to be enduring clinical trouble". Hours after the fact, witness and surveillance camera video negating the police's record started circling broadly on the web. Before the day's over, every one of the four officials was terminated.

Post-mortems

A criminal grumbling against Chauvin gave May 29, referred to significant consequences of a post-mortem directed by the Hennepin County clinical inspector, which found "no physical discoveries that help a finding of horrendous asphyxia or strangulation", yet found that Floyd experienced coronary corridor malady and hypertensive coronary illness. The grumbling referred to the post-mortem's theory that the "joined impacts of Mr Floyd being controlled by the police, his basic wellbeing conditions and any potential intoxicants in his framework likely added to his demise".

The clinical inspector's last discoveries, gave June 1, grouped Floyd's passing as a crime brought about by "a cardiopulmonary capture while being controlled" by officials who had oppressed Floyd to "neck pressure". Other critical conditions were arteriosclerotic coronary illness, hypertensive coronary illness, fentanyl inebriation, and ongoing methamphetamine use. The report expresses that on April 3 Floyd had tried positive for SARS-CoV-2, the infection that causes COVID-19, yet doesn't show it as a deadly or other noteworthy condition.

Floyd's family dispatched a subsequent post-mortem examination, completed by Michael Baden, a pathologist and previous New York City boss clinical inspector who had autopsied Eric Garner, and went to by Allecia Wilson, chief of dissection and legal administrations at the University of Michigan Medical School He found that the "proof is steady with mechanical asphyxia as the reason" of Floyd's demise", and that the passing was a crime. He said Floyd passed on from "asphyxia because of the pressure of the neck", influencing "bloodstream and oxygen going into the mind", and from "pressure of the back, which meddles with relaxing". He said Floyd had no hidden clinical issue that caused or added to his demise, and that having the option to talk doesn't imply that somebody can relax.

State criminal accusations

Chauvin was captured on May 29, Hennepin County lawyer Mike Freeman accused him of third-degree murder and second-degree homicide, making him the central white official in Minnesota to be charged in the demise of a dark regular citizen. Under Minnesota law, third-degree murder is characterized as making another's demise without expectation slaughter; however, "manifesting a debased psyche, without respect for human life". Second-degree murder likewise doesn't infer deadly plan, however, that the culprit made "a preposterous hazard" of substantial damage or passing.

On 31st May, Minnesota Attorney General Keith Ellison assumed control over the case in line with Governor Tim Walz. On June 3, Ellison corrected the charges against Chauvin to incorporate accidental second-degree murder under the crime murder teaching, asserting that Chauvin killed Floyd throughout ambushing an exhaustive round of questioning; Minnesota condemning rules suggest 12.5 years detainment on conviction of that charge. Ellison likewise charged the other three officials with supporting and abetting second-degree murder.

Government examinations

On May 26, the FBI reported it was assessing the episode, in line with the Minneapolis Police Department. On 28th May, the US Department of Justice discharged a joint explanation with the FBI, saying they had examined Floyd's passing "a top need". They said they had relegated experienced examiners and FBI criminal agents to the issue. They sketched out the examination's subsequent stages: a "far-reaching examination will assemble all accessible data and completely assess proof and data got from witnesses ... On the chance that it is resolved that there has been an infringement of government law, criminal allegations will be looked for". The Wall Street Journal ordered this announcement from the Justice Department as "quite solid", given that the division "frequently takes an increasingly quieted tone in portraying proceeding with examinations".

State social liberties activity

The Minnesota Department of Human Rights, an authoritative organization of the state, opened a social liberties examination concerning the acts of the Minneapolis Police Department on June 2. One prompt outcome was an assent order with the city; on June 5, the Minneapolis City Council approved the chairman to go into a transitory limiting request with the State of Minnesota restricting strangleholds and requiring cops to intercede against the utilization of unnecessary power by different officials. The civic chairman brought the application into power that day.

Dedications and fights

The region around the area at which Floyd was murdered turned into an improvised remembrance all through May 26, with numerous bulletins paying tribute to him and referencing the Black Lives Matter development. As the day advanced, more individuals appeared at show against Floyd's passing. The group, assessed to be in the several individuals, at that point walked to the Third Precinct of the Minneapolis Police. Members utilized banners and mottos with expressions, for example, "Equity for George", "I can't breathe", and "Black Lives Matter".

The fights were at first quiet, yet later there was vandalism of stores; at the third Precinct police headquarters windows were broken and fires set. This prompted cops in revolt gear utilizing nerve gas and glimmer explosives on the dissenters, while a few dissidents tossed rocks and different articles at the police. The police likewise used elastic slugs and smoke bombs against the nonconformists. The media has featured the bright contrasts in hostility between the police reaction to dark dissidents in these fights versus the more estimated response to the 2020 United States against lockdown fights including firearm using white nonconformists. This feeling additionally spread via web-based networking media. On May 28, it was accounted for that more than 170 organizations were plundered or harmed in Minneapolis' neighboring city of St. Paul.

While tranquil fights proceeded, others again got vicious after dusk, with the example rehashing for a few days. As of June 2, the Star Tribune evaluated 308 organizations in the Minneapolis–St. Paul region had been vandalized or annihilated, remembering 41 for Minneapolis and 3 in St. Paul devastated by fire.

Following the revolting, an evening check-in time in Minneapolis–Saint Paul and Dakota County were set up on May 29. 500 Minnesota National Guard officers were later dispatched to the region to uphold the time limitation, however to little impact, with around 1,000 nonconformists having the option to walk calmly on Interstate 35 well into check-in time.

An open commemoration, with Reverend Al Sharpton conveying the tribute, was held June 4 at North Central University in Minneapolis. A public review and a family commemoration were held in Raeford, North Carolina on June 6, close to Floyd's old neighborhood. Raeford is additionally where his sister lives. Floyd's family designs an open dedication in Houston on June 8 and private assistance on June 9. The family said proficient fighter Floyd Mayweather would pay for the administrations.

Fights requesting equity for George Floyd, now and again likewise to show against issues with police severity in their nations, occurred more than 100 urban communities, including New York City; Los Angeles; Chicago; Toronto; Mashhad; Milan;

Columbus, Ohio; Denver; Des Moines; Houston; Louisville; Memphis; Charlotte, North Carolina; Oakland; Portland, Oregon; San Jose; Seattle; outside the White House in Washington; outside Chauvin's late spring home in Windermere, Florida; and in numerous different areas. On 30th May, 12 states called up the National Guard, and in any event, 12 significant urban communities forced curfews on Saturday night.

The timeframe that Chauvin had his knee on Floyd's neck, eight minutes forty-six seconds, was regularly observed on fight signs and messages just like the words "I can't relax".

Responses on George's murder

Loved ones

Floyd's cousin, Tera Brown, said police "should be there to serve and to secure and I didn't see a solitary one of them make the slightest effort to help while he was asking for his life effectively." One of Floyd's siblings stated: "They could have tased him; they could have maced him. Rather, they put their knee in his neck and just sat on him and afterwards continued. They rewarded him more awful than they treat creatures." Floyd's sibling, Philonese, called for harmony and stated, "Everyone has a great deal of torment at present, that is the reason this is going on, I'm worn out on observing dark individuals passing on."

Floyd's long-term companion, previous expert ball player Stephen Jackson, communicated outrage and trouble, saying video of Floyd's passing "simply pulverized me". Floyd's sweetheart, Courtney Ross, requested the network to react to his demise such that praises him: "You can't battle fire with fire. Everything just consumes, and I've seen it throughout the day – individuals hate, they're despising, they're detesting, they're frantic. What's more, he would not need that." Selwyn Jones, the sibling of Floyd's mom, said that what upset him more than anything was "hearing him [on video] require my sister".

Political responses

Minneapolis and Minnesota

Minneapolis City Councilor Andrea Jenkins, who spoke to Ward 8, where Floyd's passing happened, was cited as saying: "My heart is bleeding with sorrow for the grievous death toll the previous evening close to 38th and Chicago. Our people group keeps on being damaged once more, and over and over. We should request answers." On 26th May, Minnesota Governor Tim Walz, and Lt. Senator Peggy Flanagan requested equity and called the video "upsetting". Walz explained, "The absence of humanity in this upsetting video is sickening. We will find solutions and look for equity".

Minneapolis city hall leader Jacob Frey stated: "Being dark in America ought not to be capital punishment. For five minutes, we watched an official white press his knee into a dark man's neck ... At the point when you hear somebody calling for help, you should help. This official bombed in the most fundamental, human sense." The day after Floyd's passing, the Mayor called the end of the reacting officials "the correct call". Two days after Floyd's passing, Mayor Frey featured the racial idea of Floyd's demise and called for Chauvin to be criminally charged: "If the vast majority, especially non-white individuals, had done what a cop did late Monday, they'd as of now be in the slammer. That is the reason today I'm approaching Hennepin County Attorney Mike Freeman to charge the capturing official for this situation."

In a meeting with CBS that night, Frey was asked: "Do you feel that was murder?" He answered: "I do."

Agent Ilhan Omar, of Minnesota's fifth congressional area (which incorporates Minneapolis), required a government examination, saying: "It is sickening to watch this dark man be slaughtered while defenselessly asking for help." She later included: "The cop who executed George Floyd ought to be accused of homicide." Senator Tina Smith and Governor Tim Walz additionally called for guaranteed activity. Congressperson Amy Klobuchar responded on the next day, saying: "We heard his rehashed calls for help. We heard him state again and again that he was unable to relax.

Furthermore, presently we have seen one more astonishing and horrible occasion of an African American man biting the dust." She required the announcement on "a total and careful outside examination concerning what happened, and those engaged with this occurrence must be considered responsible." However, as a previous Hennepin County lawyer, she was reprimanded for declining to squeeze criminal allegations against police during her 8-years in the office, including against Chauvin; some required her renunciation from the Senate.

On 5ht June, after the Minneapolis City Council prohibited police strangleholds, Walz called for comparative enactment to be upheld in other Minnesota people group.

On June 7, a veto-evidence more significant part of Minneapolis city gathering vowed to disband the city's police officers. Councilman Jeremiah Ellison, who is among the individuals who support dismantling the Minneapolis Police Department, did anyway recognize that such activity would be impeded by the city sanction and may require polling form endorsement. The Minneapolis city contract gives the Minneapolis chairman "total force" over the Minneapolis Police Department.

Government

President Donald Trump sent his sympathies two days after the fact utilizing Twitter, saying he mentioned that the FBI direct a careful examination. He included, "My heart goes out to George's loved ones. Equity will be served!" Trump likewise depicted Floyd's demise as "miserable and lamentable".

On May 29, President Trump decried revolting, savagery and plundering happening during across the nation dissents, tweeting: "These THUGS are shaming the memory of George Floyd, and I won't let that occur. Just addressed Governor Tim Walz and revealed to him that the Military is with him as far as possible. Any trouble and we will expect control to be that as it may, when the plundering beginnings, the shooting begins. Much thanks to you!" On June 1, because of proceeded with fights, President Trump took steps to convey the military by summoning the Insurrection Act of 1807. U.S. ministers in the

Democratic Republic of the Congo, Kenya, Tanzania, and China communicated concern and censured the executing.

Previous U.S. presidents

All living previous United States presidents have discharged proclamations in response to the murdering of George Floyd:

On May 29, Barack Obama distributed a great proclamation through Twitter requiring "another ordinary" that parts of the bargains "extremism and inconsistent treatment". On June 3, Obama tended to Americans in a Zoom video gathering sorted out by My Brother's Keeper Alliance, a piece of the Obama Foundation. The group was titled, "Rethinking Policing in the Wake of Continued Police Violence." In the location, he stated, "this nation was established on the fight: it is known as the American Revolution, and each progression of progress in this nation, each development of opportunity, each outflow of our most profound standards has been won through endeavors that made the state of affairs awkward."

On May 30, Bill Clinton discharged an announcement utilizing the Clinton Foundation saying: "In the days since George Floyd's demise, it is unimaginable not to feel sorrow for his family — and outrage, repugnance, and disappointment that his passing is the most recent in a long queue of catastrophe and bad form, and an agonizing update that an individual's race despite everything decides how they will be treated in about each part of American life."

On June 2, George W. Bramble and previous First Lady, Laura Bush, gave a 500-word proclamation which read to some degree that they are "anguished by the ruthless suffocation of George Floyd and upset by the foul play and dread that choke out our nation", and that "It is the ideal opportunity for America to look at our appalling disappointments."

The announcement kept, saying: "Many uncertainties the equity of our nation, and in light of current circumstances. Dark individuals see the rehashed infringement of their privileges without a dire and sufficient reaction from American foundations. We realize that enduring equity will just drop by serene methods."

On June 3, Jimmy Carter and previous First Lady Rosalynn Carter likewise discharged an announcement, which read partially: "Individuals of intensity, benefit, and good still, the small voice must stand up and state 'no more' to a racially oppressive police and equity framework, unethical financial inconsistencies among whites and blacks, and government activities that subvert our brought together majority rules system."

State and neighborhood police association

The neighborhood police association communicated backing of the officials in question, saying: "The Police Officers Federation of Minneapolis will offer full help to the included officials." They likewise encouraged people in general to resist the urge to panic, saying: "Presently isn't an ideal opportunity to hurry to judgment and promptly censure our officials." Bob Kroll called Floyd a "savage crook" and said that dissidents were fear mongers. The Minnesota AFL decried Kroll–CIO, the Minneapolis part of the American Federation of State, County and Municipal Employees and the Minneapolis Federation of Teachers for his remarks on Floyd's demise, with every one of the three associations requiring his renunciation. The Minnesota Chiefs of Police Association hailed Minneapolis Chief Arradondo's quick terminating of the officials in question.

National

Police the nation over were strongly suspicious of Chauvin's activities. Pioneers from associations which incorporate many cops censured the four officials' direct. National Association of Police Organizations Executive Director William Johnson called the episode unfortunate. It stated: "I don't have the foggiest idea about the whole story, yet I can't perceive any lawful avocation, any self-preservation defence, or any ethical support." Fraternal Order of Police President Patrick Yoes said specialists must guarantee equity is served in Floyd's passing, "whatever the results".

Police boss relationship from the nation over-communicated alarm at Floyd's treatment. The heads of the International Association of Chiefs of Police and the Major Cities Chiefs Association criticized what was seen on the video. The MCCA drove by Houston Police Chief Art Acevedo, stated: "The demise of Mr Floyd is profoundly upsetting and ought to be of worry to all Americans. The official's activities are conflicting with the preparation and conventions of our calling and MCCA compliments Minneapolis Police Chief Medaria Arradondo for his quick and definitive activity to fire the work of the officials in question." The National Police Foundation President stated: "These activities, and inaction, endanger the increases that have been made through the penances and fearlessness of many." Leaders of individual police divisions from around the United States stood in opposition to the official at the focal point of the video, with what The Washington Post called "sicken", and the Los Angeles Times called "gruff analysis". The LA Times stated: "It was an uncommon second when police pioneers were unequivocal in their open hatred for the direction of one of their own." Leaders denouncing the official's activities incorporated the New York City Police Commissioner, the Sheriffs of Los Angeles and San Diego areas, and the Police Chiefs of Los Angeles, Boston, Miami, Houston, and Austin, just as a previous Police Chief from Seattle. Police head of littler urban communities stood up also: Chiefs of Police from Buffalo Grove, Illinois; Tucson, Arizona; Round Rock, Texas; the University of Texas at Austin; Pflugerville, Texas; and Omaha, Nebraska; all gave articulations against Floyd's treatment. An appointee sheriff in Jones County, Mississippi was terminated for posting via web-based networking media: "On the off chance that he can shout he can breathe [sic], something different was going on."

Organizations

The University of Minnesota declared that it would be constraining binds with the Minneapolis Police Department and that it would no longer agreement the nearby police division for help at significant occasions. The Minneapolis School Board passed goals at its gathering on June 2, ending its relationship with the Minneapolis Police Department. The Walker Art Center and the Minneapolis Institute of Art reported on June 3 that they would no longer agreement Minneapolis Police Department officials for security at their exhibition hall occasions.

On 5ht June, the United States Marine Corps declared it would no longer approve any open showcase of a Confederate banner on any office or establishment. "Recent developments are an obvious update that it isn't sufficient for us to evacuate images that cause division – rather, we additionally should endeavor to wipe out division itself," said Gen. David H. Berger, Commandant of the Marine Corps

Global Nations and associations

Canada: Canadian Prime Minister Justin Trudeau said that racism was genuine and existed in both the United States and Canada. He at that point encouraged Canadians to face it.

China: The Foreign Ministry of China condemned the executing of George Floyd with the announcement: "The demise of George Floyd mirrors the seriousness of racial separation and police fierceness in the US", and encouraged the US to "dispense with racial segregation and secure the legal privileges of minorities". State media ran critical inclusion of the occasions, intending to feature what Foreign Ministry representative Zhao Lijian called a "twofold norm" contrasted with US reprobation of police ruthlessness in the 2019–20 Hong Kong fights.

Germany: Chancellor Angela Merkel depicted the police activity as murder saying: "this homicide of George Floyd is something extremely, horrible".

Iran: Iran's Supreme Leader, Ali Khamenei, retweeted a tweet saying individuals with brown complexion confronted being killed "in the following couple of moments" on the off chance that they left American roads. Remote Ministry representative Abbas Mousavi approached the US to "stop abuse and forceful behaviours against its kin and let them relax".

Ireland: Irish Taoiseach Leo Varadkar has said that there is a "nonattendance of the good initiative" in the US following the passing of George Floyd.

Peru: Peruvian President Martín Vizcarra communicated that the executing of Floyd is "an indication of racism and segregation" that must be dismissed. He said that as indicated by what was replied in the last national registration, over half of Peruvians felt separated sooner or later in their lives. At last, he saluted the Afro-Peruvian people group on the Day of Afro-Peruvian Culture.

Russia: The Russian Ministry of Foreign Affairs said the US had a past filled with orderly human rights mishandles.

South Africa: The African National Congress, the administering party in South Africa, discharged an announcement calling for quiet in the U.S., which was condemned for not referencing comparable passings because of police activity in South Africa.

Turkey: Turkish President Recep Tayyip Erdoğan accused Floyd's demise of a "supremacist and fundamentalist methodology" by the United States and said Turkey would screen the issue while stretching out sympathies to his family and friends and family.

Joined Kingdom: British Prime Minister Boris Johnson said that "supremacist savagery has no spot in our general public", and that he was "dismayed and sickened" by the recording. He additionally asked individuals to "fight calmly and as per the principles on social separating".

Venezuela: Venezuelan President Nicolás Maduro blamed President Trump for utilizing the U.S. military against his kin and guaranteed that demonstrators are rioting requesting a conclusion to racism and police savagery.

Global associations

African Union: African Union authorities, including Moussa Faki Mahamat, the executive of the African Union Commission, reprimanded the slaughtering. U.S. international safe havens in Africa additionally denounced the episode, in a move that was depicted by the media as strange.

European Union: Josep Borrell, the EU's international strategy boss, said the alliance is "stunned and dismayed" by the demise of dark American George Floyd in police authority, calling it "maltreatment of intensity" and notice against further over the top utilization of power.

Joined Nations: Michelle Bachelet, the United Nations High Commissioner for Human Rights, denounced it up 'til now another slaughtering of an unarmed African American and approached the United States to take "genuine activity" and end the rehash of such killings. She likewise asked protestors to "express their requests for equity calmly" and for police to abstain from further utilization of unreasonable power. On June 5, 2020, a gathering of 66 UN specialists called the passing of George Floyd as present-day "racial fear" lynching in the US. "African Americans keep on encountering racial dread in state-supported and secretly composed brutality. In the US, this heritage of racial dread stays clear in present-day policing," the gathering of specialists cited.

Strict pioneers

The Dalai Lama, in India, while showing understudies, censured the slaughtering of George Floyd by saying, "there are some who even accept it as a pride to have the option to murder someone".

Pope Francis tended to Floyd's demise during his week by week petition at the Vatican on June 3: "Dear siblings and sisters in the United States, I have seen with extraordinary concern the upsetting social agitation in your country in these previous days, following the lamentable passing of Mr George Floyd." He included: "We can't endure or deliberately ignore racism and avoidance in any structure but guarantee to safeguard the holiness of each human life."

Reactions of neck limitations

Minneapolis cops have a record of directing neck restrictions, in any event, multiple times since the start of 2015. This incorporates 44 individuals who were rendered oblivious. A few law implementation experts said the quantity of unaware people because of this move appears to be astoundingly enormous. Police characterize neck limitations as "when an official uses an arm or leg to pack somebody's neck without straightforwardly compelling the aviation route". The utilization of the stranglehold move known as a "neck restriction" has been mocked by over twelve law authorization authorities, who were met by NBC News. The news association gave a summation of their perspectives: "The specific strategy Chauvin utilized – stooping on a speculate's neck – is neither instructed nor endorsed by any police organization." A Minneapolis city official stated: "Chauvin's strategy isn't allowed by the Minneapolis police officer." by and large, police divisions' utilization of arranged kinds of neck restrictions, depicted as strangling holds, are wholly outlined – if not unlawful.

Applying a knee tightly to the neck of an individual lying on their stomach (inclined position) isn't suggested by law implementation experts because doing so can bring about suffocation. Simultaneously, keeping an individual in a likely situation, with hands handcuffed despite his good faith is intended to be of exceptionally brief span and is viewed as unsafe because breathing is promptly confined in that position. "Somebody in that position can attract enough breath to heave or talk in sprays, yet they can't inhale completely, so they bit by bit lose oxygen and fall oblivious." The individual must be immediately moved on his side, sat up, or held up. Weight on a prisoner's neck can "cause deadly harm" so the movie must be observed intently for the prosperity of the prisoner. As indicated by the Minneapolis office's manual, particular preparing is required to utilize this move. As noted in the Minneapolis police approach, this move must be used if all else fails when there is no other method to repress a presume who is antagonistically opposing capture. Chauvin's activities may have surpassed his domain.

Scholarly specialists on the utilization of power by police censured Chauvin's activities. Mylan Masson, a long-lasting Minneapolis cop and previous chief of the Hennepin Technical College's Law Enforcement and Criminal Justice Center, which trains roughly 50% of Minnesota's cops, said a type of the procedure found in the video of Floyd's demise was instructed until in any event 2016. He included: "Once the [officer] is in charge, at that point, you discharge. That is the thing that utilization of power is: you use it until the danger has halted." George Kirkham, a previous cop and educator emeritus at Florida State University's College of Criminology and Criminal Justice, stated: "It was crazy, over the top, an outlandish power considering the present situation. We're managing a guilty property party. The man was inclined on the ground. He was no danger to anybody." Seth Stoughton, a partner teacher of law at the University of South Carolina, who was likewise a previous cop, said that putting presumes lying face-down with their hands bound behind their backs for a significant period was risky because it gambled positional asphyxia. On the off chance that a suitable place their knee on a speculate's neck in this position, it could cause injury or even demise.

Memorial service of George Floyd

Individuals from the open will be permitted to see his body for 6 hours on Monday, June 8, in Floyd's old neighborhood of Houston. Thousands are relied upon to see the collection. A private memorial service for George Floyd will be hung on Tuesday, June 9. Previous Vice President and 2020 Democratic chosen one Joe Biden will meet with the Floyd family secretly and give a video message at the burial service. Floyd will be covered close to his mom in Pearland, Texas.

Conclusions: How to end racism?

Racism is the point at which somebody is dealt with contrastingly on account of their race or culture. It can incorporate things like calling individuals names or barring them and in any event, denying them administration at a business or something like openings for work. It's unlawful in the UK to victimize (treat quickly) somebody on account of their race. If you or somebody you know is encountering racism, you can find support to make this stop.

Try not to take the maltreatment.
Everybody, regardless of what their nationality or race is, has an option to live joyfully and liberated from separation. On the off chance that you feel somebody's bigot towards you, Childline has data about what steps you can take. The primary concern is to leave, be careful and converse with somebody you trust. You don't have to fight back or react.

If you feel you've been oppressed unlawfully, for instance, grinding away or by a business, you can discover your privileges at Citizens Advice. If somebody is supremacist towards you, the most significant thing is your wellbeing. On the off chance that you feel helpless, stay with gatherings of companions you trust, on the chance that you or somebody you know is in quick or dangerous peril, dial 999. Keep in mind; you're not the one raising a ruckus. You've done nothing incorrectly.

Keep proof

Keep a journal of what's been occurring and spare any writings or messages to show others how it is influencing you and what bolster you need. If you make a move, any proof you can assemble will support your case.

Tell somebody

Address your instructors, youth labourers, companions as well as a family about what's happening with the goal that you can get their assistance and backing. In case you don't know how to begin the discussion, Childline has valuable data about how to approach a grown-up for help.

Report it

You can report supremacist occurrences to Police Scotland by visiting your neighborhood police headquarters, rounding out an online structure. Resident's Advice Scotland has more data about what happens when you report an occurrence, what data you'll be requested and what may occur after the episode has been accounted for. At the point when you say the event, you ought to seek the episode reference number. On the off chance that you experience issues talking or getting English, you can request that the police give a translator - they should provide you with one.

Keep in mind: you don't need to be the race or culture that somebody has expected you are the point at which they state or plan something for you with the goal for it to be a detest wrongdoing or occurrence. Discover progressively about hate wrongdoing and episodes and how to report them.

Remain safe on the web

In case you're encountering misuse on the web, you can generally report it utilizing the 'report misuse' button on most online networking stages. Ensure your protection settings are secure, as well. The UK Safer Internet Center has a few assets remembering guides for how to ensure every one of your web-based life accounts is private and secure.

You can likewise distinct square individuals on the off chance that they're irritating or harassing you. We have a guide on the best way to square individuals on each internet-based life stage. The foundation Glitch has a valuable asset to assist you with recording any online maltreatment which can be utilized as proof if you later make a report to the police.

Get others included

Only discussing racism is a significant piece of battling it. You could begin an enemy of racism venture or bulletin at your school/youth gathering or set up a conversation gathering to discuss relevant issues and what you can do to help.

Never surrender!

You probably won't have the option to handle racism without anyone else; however, we would all be able to have an impact. Testing racism when you see it (without putting yourself in danger) and revealing it assists with making others see it's not alright.

Bolster others

On the off chance that you see or hear somebody being supremacist towards another person, you can assist with supporting that individual. Directly inquiring as to whether they're alright and telling them that what you saw wasn't right can genuinely help. You could assist them with reporting it on the off chance that they need and offer to be an observer. This is called Third Party Reporting.

If you feel good and the circumstance implies it's protected to do as such, you can likewise challenge racism when you see it by saying you don't concur with it.

Activity on Prejudice has an asset, called Speak Up, to assist you with seeing how you can be what is called a functioning observer, this implies when somebody sees struggle or unsatisfactory conduct they make strides that can have any kind of effect in a sheltered and fitting manner.

CPSIA information can be obtained
at www.ICGtesting.com
Printed in the USA
LVHW050131070121
675887LV00019B/2756